THE BIBLICAL HEART

Terry Busler

The Biblical Heart

Published by
Tremendous Leadership
P.O. Box 267
Boiling Springs, PA 17007

1-800-233-2665
www.tremendousleadership.com

Artwork by Jerry Anderson
www.jandersonart.com

Scripture used is KJV unless otherwise noted.
Definitions throughout are based on Websters Dictionary 1828, but edited through the lens of the author's experience.

Printed in the United States of America

ISBN 978-1-949033-20-5

TABLE OF CONTENTS

ACKNOWLEDGEMENTS

I dedicate this book, first and foremost to my Lord and Savior, Jesus Christ, who will bring about my ultimate healing in this lifetime or in heaven; to the Christian counselor who helped me come to salvation, and who God used greatly in my emotional healing. I was truly emotionally damaged. I leave this book as a legacy to my children. Special thanks to my mother, father, wife, brother, sister, and my two sons and daughter, who each helped give me ideas for the book and whom I love very much. I also acknowledge my brother-in-law and his second wife (my sister died in her forties). He is a true gentleman and his wife, very gracious. I also give thanks to my doctors: my family doctor, my foot care specialist, my podiatrist, my psychologist, my psychiatrists, and my endocrinologist. Also, the hospital and rehabilitation facilities were amazing and renewed my physical health and well-being. I am also grateful for my employer. On an impulse, I went to management for help and they referred me to a Christian psychologist.

FOREWORD

In my experience of having both Diabetes and Bipolar disorder, the symptoms can be very similar. One of the symptoms is mood swings, such as sudden anger and rage. I will dive deeper into these issues in the book. I bring up my physical condition to share with the reader so they understand how the scripture can be used to help you through this.

You will see how these health challenges affected my life and the lives of those around me, however, God's living word is able to conquer any affliction. Below is some helpful information which reveals how widespread and common these illnesses are.

Hyperglycemia (High blood sugar)

Hypoglycemia (Low blood sugar)

Diabetes[1]
1. Common Symptoms: Uncleanness of hygiene, lack of order, anger/irritability, rage/wrath. (While I personally didn't experience rage/wrath, this is a symptom many do experience.)
2. Diabetics are often treated by Endocrinologists or family doctors
3. Undiagnosed: 30.3 million adults.

---

[1] Prevalence of Diagnosed Diabetes | National Diabetes Statistics Report | Data & Statistics | Diabetes | CDC. (n.d.). Retrieved from https://www.cdc.gov/diabetes/data/statistics-report/diagnosed.html

4. Diagnosed: 23.1 million (1.5 million diagnosed newly every year).
5. 193,000 children and adolescents under the age of 20 are diagnosed diabetics.
6. Diagnosis by Race: (Americans, US)
   a. Whites (7.4%)
   b. Asian (8.0%)
   c. Hispanics (12.1%)
   d. Blacks (12.7%)
   e. Indians/Alaskan Natives (15.1%)
7. Deaths: In 2015: 252,806 death certificates listing diabetes as an underlying or contributing cause of death, and 79,535 death certificates listing it as the underlying cause of death.

"And God saw that the wickedness of man was great in the earth, and that every imagination of the thoughts of his heart was only evil continually." (*King James Version*, Genesis 6:5)

"Blessed is the man that walketh not in the counsel of the ungodly, nor standeth in the way of sinners, nor sitteth in the seat of the scornful." (Psalm 1:1)

There is a crisis in America regarding mental illness, drug and alcohol abuse. Here are the 2018 statistics. There are 1000 chapters of NAMI in the US. I had a difficult time finding a Christian psychiatrist in my area.

Mental Health[2]
- Approximately 1 in 5 adults in the U.S. (46.6 million) experiences mental illness in a given year.
- Approximately 1 in 25 adults in the U.S. (11.2 million) experiences a serious mental illness in a given year that substantially interferes with or limits one or more major life activities.

---

[2]NAMI. (n.d.). Retrieved from https://www.nami.org/learn-more/mental-health-by-the-numbers

- Approximately 1 in 5 youth aged 13–18 (21.4%) experiences a severe mental disorder at some point during their life. For children aged 8–15, the estimate is 13%.
- 1.1% of adults in the U.S. live with schizophrenia.
- 2.6% of adults in the U.S. live with bipolar disorder.
- 6.9% of adults in the U.S.—16 million—had at least one major depressive episode in the past year.
- 18.1% of adults in the U.S. experienced an anxiety disorder such as posttraumatic stress disorder, obsessive-compulsive disorder and specific phobias.
- Among the 20.2 million adults in the U.S. who experienced a substance use disorder, 50.5%—10.2 million adults—had a co-occurring mental illness.
- An estimated 26% of homeless adults staying in shelters live with serious mental illness and an estimated 46% live with severe mental illness and/or substance use disorders.
- Approximately 20% of state prisoners and 21% of local jail prisoners have "a recent history" of a mental health condition.
- 70% of youth in juvenile justice systems have at least one mental health condition and at least 20% live with a serious mental illness.
- Only 41% of adults in the U.S. with a mental health condition received mental health services in the past year. Among adults with a serious mental illness, 62.9% received mental health services in the past year
- Just over half (50.6%) of children with a mental health condition aged 8-15 received mental health services in the previous year.
- African Americans and Hispanic Americans each use mental health services at about one-half the rate of Caucasian Americans and Asian Americans at about one-third the rate.
- Half of all chronic mental illness begins by age 14; three-quarters by age 24. Despite effective treatment, there are long delays—sometimes decades—between the first appearance of symptoms and when people get help.

- Serious mental illness costs America $193.2 billion in lost earnings per year.
- Mood disorders, including major depression, dysthymic disorder and bipolar disorder, are the third most common cause of hospitalization in the U.S. for both youth and adults aged 18–44.
- Individuals living with serious mental illness face an increased risk of having chronic medical conditions. Adults in the U.S. living with serious mental illness die on average 25 years earlier than others, largely due to treatable medical conditions.
- Over one-third (37%) of students with a mental health condition age 14–21 and older who are served by special education drop out—the highest dropout rate of any disability group.
- Suicide is the 10th leading cause of death in the U.S., and the 2nd leading cause of death for people aged 10–34.
- More than 90% of people who die by suicide show symptoms of a mental health condition.
- Each day an estimated 18-22 veterans die by suicide.

INTRODUCTION

I feel God inspired me to write, *The Biblical Heart: Emotions, Mind, Spirit, and Healing*, from a biblical perspective that I might help others who have experienced, are experiencing, or will experience the same feelings I have had in my life. As you work your way through this book, you will have the opportunity to better understand how the Bible frames the reality of your emotions, your mind, your spirit, and how to heal. While the definitions are pulled from Websters Dictionary 1828, I have edited them to include the understanding God has inspired upon me through His word.

My journey to salvation may be briefly described as follows. Growing up, my mom and dad brought me to church. I did not get saved there but it helped. My family had a friend in Virginia who did not believe in the Bible because he felt there were too many contradictions. (After much of my own study, I found this not to be true.) In 1972, because of what this atheist said, I was motivated to start studying the Bible, so if a similar situation came up, I could provide an informed answer.

I had an emotional breakdown when three calamities occurred. In 1978, I was flooded out by Hurricane Eloise, the Three Mile Island disaster[3] occurred, and my marriage was failing. I was like

---

[3]In 1979, a malfunction at the Three Mile Island nuclear power plant resulted in venting of radioactive fumes into the surrounding Harrisburg, PA area. Due to miscommunications both within and outside of official government channels, mass uncertainty surrounding a potential evacuation of the 30,000 surrounding residents left widespread distrust and confusion, much of which lasts even today.

a vegetable. I expressed my hope that things could get better to the woman who referred me, but she assured me that the counselor she referred me to could help. I felt overwhelmed by evil and the counselor said to me, "God would be insulted if you thought evil was greater than Him."

I believe there is a God who is all-powerful, and He is a real person (one that is invisible as the Bible describes Him) but was manifested in the flesh as Jesus Christ. In 2005, my doctor helped in my attempt to come off medication, but I had another emotional breakdown. I realized then, that I could not go off my medication. A third time they tried to commit me because I was having similar symptoms, lack of doing things decently/in proper order, anger, and although the third symptom is typically wrath or rage, I never reached the last symptom.

The next crisis was my diabetes. It can have similar symptoms – unclean, irritability (anger) and rage. Both being hypoglycemic and hyperglycemia can have the same symptoms. During my journey to salvation, God impressed three scriptures on my heart. First, Mark 12:30, "And thou shalt love the Lord thy God with all thy heart, and with all thy soul, and with all thy mind, and with all thy strength: this is the first commandment." Second was Psalm 118:8, "It is better to trust in the Lord than to put confidence in man." And lastly, Hebrews 11:6, "But without faith it is impossible to please him: for he that cometh to God must believe that he is, and that he is a rewarder of them that diligently seek him." I have placed a monument in my front yard with these scriptures on it to show my love for God, with the hope that the hearts of those who read it will be touched by God as His word does not return void.

"But there is a spirit in man: and the inspiration of the Almighty giveth them understanding." (Job 32:8)

"And they overcame him by the blood of the Lamb, and by the word of their testimony; and they loved not their lives unto the death." (Revelation 12:11)

"And not only so, but we glory in tribulations also: knowing that tribulation worketh patience;" (Romans 5:3)

"And I wrote this same unto you, lest, when I came, I should have sorrow from them of whom I ought to rejoice; having confidence in you all, that my joy is the joy of you all. For out of much affliction and anguish of heart I wrote unto you with many tears; not that ye should be grieved, but that ye might know the love which I have more abundantly unto you." (2 Corinthians 2:3-4)

"These things I have spoken unto you, that in me ye might have peace. In the world ye shall have tribulation: but be of good cheer; I have overcome the world." (John 16:33)

THE EMOTIONAL BRAIN

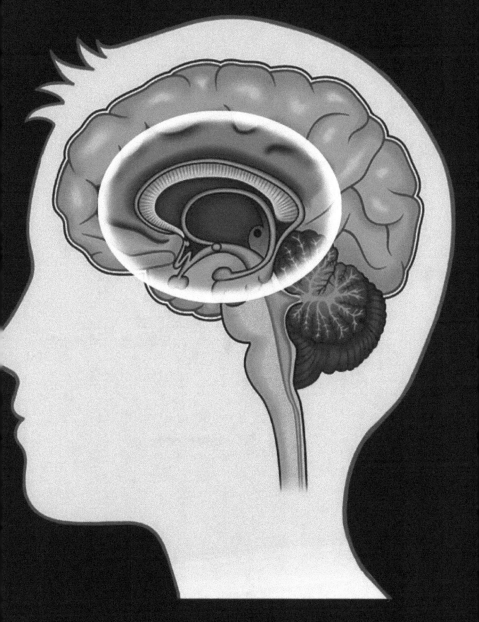

Genesis 26:35

EMOTIONS

CR

Emotions: In a philosophical sense, an internal motion or agitation of the mind which passes away without desire; when desire follows, the motion or agitation is called a passion.[1]

Passion: The sensible effect, the feeling to which the mind is subjected, when an object of importance suddenly and imperiously demands its attention. The state of absolute passiveness, in consequence of any sudden percussion of mind, is of short duration. The strong impression, or vivid sensation, immediately produces a reaction correspondent to its nature, either to appropriate and enjoy, or avoid and repel the exciting cause. This reaction is very properly distinguished by the term *emotion.*

Feelings: Instantaneous reactions to an external stimuli. Lasting satisfaction and joy can only come from the Lord.

"Which were a grief of mind unto Isaac and to Rebekah." (Genesis 26:35)

---

[1]Websters Dictionary 1828. (n.d.). *Websters Dictionary 1828 – American Dictionary of the English Language.* [online] Available at: http://websters dictionary1828.com/

"But the LORD said unto Samuel, Look not on his countenance, or on the height of his stature; because I have refused him: for the LORD seeth not as man seeth; for man looketh on the outward appearance, but the LORD looketh on the heart." (1 Samuel 16:7)

"A merry heart maketh a cheerful countenance: but by sorrow of the heart the spirit is broken." (Proverbs 15:13)

"Thou hast given him his heart's desire, and hast not withholden the request of his lips..." (Psalm 21:2)

What we bring into our minds is critical. It is also important to recognize what we are feeling and how those feelings affect our thoughts and words. An emotion or feeling is only part of the picture, but a very important part. Any action thereafter should be based on the feeling, our thoughts, and much prayer.

In the book entitled, *More Leadership Lessons of Jesus: A Timeless Model for Today's Leaders*, there is a chapter entitled, Guard your Heart. In this chapter, authors Ray Pritchard and Bob Briner build a good case that we should guard what we bring into our minds; "An effective leader guards his own heart because everything important comes out of it." Both Mark 7:15 and Proverbs 4:23 state above all else to guard your heart for it is the wellspring of life. Proverbs 23:7 says, "For as he thinketh in his heart, so is he." Psalm 101:3 says, "I will set no wicked thing before mine eyes: I hate the work of them that turn aside; it shall not cleave to me."

Wicked things in today's world deeply effect our hearts and our actions. Pornography, movies about witchcraft, astrology, and most of today's television shows are not what we should place in our hearts. Many times I would come away from watching TV feeling angry or down due to the content. I recommend you not go to R- or X-rated movies. Even some PG-13 movies are questionable. Listen to Christian reviews before going to the movies. Read primarily Christian books and listen to Christian radio. Philippians 4:8 says, "Finally, brethren, whatsoever things are true, whatsoever things are honest, whatsoever things are just, whatsoever things are pure, whatsoever things are lovely, whatsoever things are of good report; if there be any virtue, and if there be any praise, think on these things." If we see or hear something, it is inevitable we will think about it at some point and time and with those thoughts will also come feelings.

Here are some other Scriptures about the heart pertaining to emotions and my findings through them:

"And supper being ended, the devil having now put into the heart of Judas Iscariot, Simon's son, to betray him;" (John 13:2)

If we open up our heart to evil influences, God may lift His hand of protection and allow the devil to influence and affect our hearts. If we don't know the Lord as our Savior and have a personal relationship with Him, God may even allow the devil to possess our hearts.

"For God maketh my heart soft, and the Almighty troubleth me: Because I was not cut off before the darkness, neither hath he covered the darkness from my face." (Job 23:16-17)

God can bring dark feelings and emotions into our lives to bring us closer to Him.

"My flesh and my heart faileth: but God is the strength of my heart, and my portion forever." (Psalm 73:26)

"And he said unto them, Ye are they which justify yourselves before men; but God knoweth your hearts: for that which is highly esteemed among men is abomination in the sight of God." (Luke 16:15)

Be not deceived. God knows our hearts. Nothing is hidden from Him.

Affliction

Affliction: The state of being afflicted; a state of pain, distress, or grief. The cause of continued pain of body or mind, as sickness, losses, calamity, adversity, persecution.

Anguish: Extreme pain, either of body or mind. As pain of the mind, it signifies any keen distress from sorrow, remorse, despair and kindred passions.

Distress: Extreme pain; anguish of body or mind; as, to suffer great distress from the gout or loss of near friends. To afflict greatly; to harass; to oppress with calamity; to make miserable.

Misery: Great unhappiness; extreme pain of body or mind; a man suffers misery from the gout, or from great afflictions, distress, calamity and other evils.

Miserable: Very unhappy from grief, pain, calamity, poverty, apprehension of evil, or other causes. What hopes delude thee, miserable man?

> "Many are the afflictions of the righteous: but the LORD delivereth him out of them all." (Psalm 34:19)

> "The Lord redeemeth the soul of his servants: and none of them that trust in him shall be desolate." (Psalm 34:22)

> "The Lord is nigh (near) to them that are of a broken heart; and saveth such as be of a contrite (humble) spirit." (Psalm 34:18)

One of the groups of people that experience affliction, who I hope someday to minister to, is our godly politicians/government officials. I witnessed what I call a grilling by Congress of Donald Rumsfeld over the improper/scandalous way Iraqi prisoners were interrogated in prison in Iraq. The interrogation of Rumsfeld by Congress had to cause him pain of mind, affliction, distress, misery. My heart went out to him. Another example was the interrogation of Brett Kavanaugh who was attempting to become a Supreme Court Justice. Both handled the questions courageously and humbly. "All men have sinned and fall short of the glory of God" (Romans 3:23); so no man has a completely clean past. Only by the death of Christ are we clean and forgiven. But those who oppose Christ would like to bring down godly politicians by exposing the sins of their past, causing them pain of mind through extreme embarrassment or emotional pain, even though God has forgiven those who have repented.

Other scriptures on affliction:

"Consider mine affliction, and deliver me: for I do not forget thy law." (Psalm 119:153)

"And ye became followers of us, and of the Lord, having received the word in much affliction, with joy of the Holy Ghost." (1 Thessalonians 1:6)

Anger

Anger: A state of emotional excitement induced by intense displeasure as a result of a real or imagined threat, insult, put-down, frustration or injustice to yourself or those important to you.

Frustration: The act of feeling disappointment or defeat; as the frustration of one's attempt or design.

Wrath: Violent anger; vehement exasperation; indignation.

Rage: To be furious with anger; to be exasperated to fury; to be violently agitated with passion.

> "An angry man stirreth up strife, and a furious man aboundeth in transgression." (Proverbs 29:22)

> "And when Haman saw that Mordecai bowed not, nor did him reverence, then was Haman full of wrath." (Esther 3:5)

> "And hired counsellors against them, to frustrate their purpose, all the days of Cyrus king of Persia, even until the reign of Darius king of Persia." (Ezra 4:5)

I don't believe there is any family that doesn't deal with issues of anger, so if you experience this, call yourselves 'normal.' I would like to relate a story to you in which I became very frustrated. When I look back on it, it certainly wasn't as serious as I felt.

Each year my family goes to Canada. My wife primarily packs the suitcases, gets the food ready, and generally has 80 percent of what needs to go ready for me. I, on the other hand, pack everything into the car; the canoe, the motor, the fishing gear and everything my wife has prepared. Sounds pretty equitable in the distribution of responsibilities. Here is where the problem lies. My wife packs for an expedition while I pack for an excursion. As I slowly progress through packing the car, I see I'm beginning to run out of room and it also looks like my wife is just about out of things to bring me. I'm about ready to close the trunk, as it is full when out come fifteen more items. I consider myself to be a man of average intelligence and I think to myself, 'I can handle this'. I begin to repack as the car sinks to its tire rims, with twelve more items to go. That's when the frustration begins. You can only pack so much into the car and on top of the car. By the time my wife is ready to go, I am so frustrated that I express my frustration in very gentle terms. She says let me repack things for you.

My dad could always get things in his car. He was a great packer. Maybe he could teach you a thing or two about how to pack. My boys and friends have ridden in the vehicle where they were so cramped they had to stretch their legs over the front seat for relief. My wife has stuff crammed at her feet but doesn't complain. To alleviate the car from dragging on the ground I had heavy duty springs installed. Trips to Canada, to say the least, are an adventure. I believe I've taken the kitchen sink to Canada and back but it's hard to tell with all the paraphernalia. My wife and I have come to joke now that she packs for an expedition and I pack for an excursion. That's just the way we are.

In the book entitled, *Overcoming Hurts and Anger,* author Dwight L. Carlson says, "When anger or displeasure is very great and is processed through the conscious part of the mind, it activates the fight or flight mechanism in the body, which prepares it for battle or escape. This mechanism releases adrenaline, which in turn increases the blood pressure, pulse and respiration rate."

Let's focus on methods of handling your anger. One is to suppress action until you've thought through the situation and have control of what you say and do. The Bible encourages us not to be hasty in dealing with our anger. Proverbs 29:11 says, "A fool uttereth all his mind: but a wise man keepeth it in till afterwards." A second way to handle anger is to pray. I often pray for wisdom and protection of my emotions. James 1:5 says, "If any of you lack wisdom, let him ask of God, that giveth to all men liberally, and upbraideth not; and it shall be given him." A third way to handle anger is to confront when necessary. In 2 Corinthians 2:4, Paul shared how he felt about confronting them. He said, "For out of much affliction and anguish of heart I wrote unto you with many tears; not that ye should be grieved, but that ye might know the love which I have more abundantly unto you." Ephesians 4:25-27 says, "Wherefore putting away lying, speak every man truth with his neighbour: for we are members one of another. Be ye angry, and sin not: let not the sun go down upon your wrath: Neither give place to the devil."

Apathy

Apathy: Want of feeling; an utter privation of passion, or insensibility to pain. As applied to the mind, it is stoicism (insensibility) a calmness of the mind incapable of being ruffled by pleasure, pain, or passion.

Indifference: Unconcernedness; A state of the mind when it feels no anxiety or interest in what is presented to it.

Careless: Not regarding with care; unmoved by; unconcerned for.

"Rise up, ye women that are at ease; hear my voice, ye careless daughters; give ear unto my speech." (Isaiah 32:9)

"And Joshua said unto the children of Israel, How long are ye slack to go to possess the land, which the LORD God of your fathers hath given you?" (Joshua 18:3)

"And because iniquity shall abound, the love of many shall wax cold." (Matthew 24:12)

The feelings I have as a result of the prescription dosage for being bipolar raised what could best be described as apathy, indifference, carelessness, or insensibility. I resisted this feeling as God would not want my love to wax cold. He would not want me to be apathetic, unfeeling, and careless. I prayed the drug dosage would continue to be lowered so as I could feel love once more. Thankfully, lowering the dosage of the drug is what the doctor said he would do.

Other scriptures on apathy and indifference:

"I know thy works, that thou art neither cold nor hot: I would thou wert cold or hot." (Revelation 3:15)

"Our soul is exceedingly filled with the scorning of those that are at ease, and with the contempt of the proud." (Psalm 123:4)

"Therefore hear now this, thou that art given to pleasures, that dwellest carelessly, that sayest in thine heart, I am, and none else beside me; I shall not sit as a widow, neither shall I know the loss of children:" (Isaiah 47:8)

Compassion

Compassion: A suffering with another; painful sympathy; a sensation of sorrow excited by the distress or misfortunes of another, pity; commiseration; compassion is a mixed passion, compounded of love and sorrow;

Pity: The feeling or suffering of one person excited by the distresses of another, sympathy with the grief or misery of another.

> "But when he saw the multitudes, he was moved with compassion on them, because they fainted, and were scattered abroad, as sheep having no shepherd." (Matthew 9:36)

> "And of some have compassion, making a difference:" (Jude 1:22)

> "And they remembered that God was their rock, and the high God their redeemer. Nevertheless they did flatter him with their mouth, and they lied unto him with their tongues. For their heart was not right with him, neither were they steadfast in his covenant. But he, being full of compassion, forgave their iniquity, and destroyed them not: yea, many a time turned he his anger away, and did not stir up all his wrath. For he remembered that they were but flesh; a wind that passeth away, and cometh not again." (Psalm 78:35-39)

Whenever you see your child rebel or go in the wrong direction, you feel compassion for your child. When a loved one, family or friend dies you feel sorrow or grief for that person. When you see a poor or homeless person, you feel pity. My brother, who lives in California, has great compassion for the homeless.

Other scriptures on compassion:

"Who can have compassion on the ignorant, and on them that are out of the way; for that he himself also is compassed with infirmity." (Hebrews 5:2)

"But when the young man heard that saying, he went away sorrowful: for he had great possessions." (Matthew 19:22)

"Which were a grief of mind unto Isaac and to Rebekah." (Genesis 26:35)

"When Jesus therefore saw her weeping, and the Jews also weeping which came with her, he groaned in the spirit, and was troubled. And said, Where have ye laid him? They said unto him, Lord, come and see. Jesus wept." (John 11:33-35)

Comment: Jesus had compassion for Mary and the Jews.

Cruelty

Cruelty: Inhumanity; a savage or barbarous disposition or temper, which is gratified by giving unnecessary pain or distress to others; barbarity; applied to persons; the cruelty and envy of the people. Barbarous deed; any act of a human being which inflicts unnecessary pain; any act intended to torment, vex, or afflict, or which actually torments or afflicts, without necessity; wrong; injustice; oppression.

Abusive: Containing abuse, or that is the instrument of abuse, as abusive words; rude; reproachful.

"The diseased have ye not strengthened, neither have ye healed that which was sick, neither have ye bound up that which was broken, neither have ye brought again that which was driven away, neither have ye sought that which was lost; but with force and with cruelty have ye ruled them." (Ezekiel 34:4)

"And the barbarous people shewed us no little kindness: for they kindled a fire, and received us every one, because of the present rain, and because of the cold." (Acts 28:2)

"But the Philistines took him, and put out his eyes, and brought him down to Gaza, and bound him with fetters of brass; and he did grind in the prison house." (Judges 16:21)

When I was going through the divorce process, my counselor recommended that I go to an inter-church, non-denominational ministry for singles. This ministry helps singles through the pain and hurt of divorce and provides the opportunity for fellowship to those in single life. It offers volleyball for singles every Friday night at various locations, square dancing, picnics, trips to the shore and amusement parks, Bible studies, and praise and worship. During my time in the ministry, I came across a number of people where cruelty had occurred in their lives.

There were cases of physical, mental, and emotional abuse. Matthew 19:8 says, "...because of the hardness of your hearts suffered you to put away your wives: but from the beginning it was not so." Matthew 5:32 says, "But I say unto you, That whosoever shall put away his wife saving for the cause of fornication, causeth her to commit adultery; and whosoever shall marry her that is divorced committeth adultery." In the story of the adulteress where the Pharisees were about to stone a woman for adultery, Jesus said "He that is without sin among you, let him first cast a stone at her" (John 8:7). I believe Jesus viewed the punishment for her sin to be too cruel. 1 Corinthians 7:13-16 says, "And the woman that hath a husband that believeth not, and if he be pleased to dwell with her, let her not leave him. For the unbelieving wife is sanctified by the husband; else were your children unclean; But if the unbelieving depart, let him depart". A brother and sister are not in bondage in such cases but God has called us to peace.

Jesus in Matthew 19:8 was dispelling the concept that a person can divorce for any reason. The culture at that time was so lenient on reasons for divorce and cruel in other areas. Jesus tried to bring a righteous balance back to their culture. Pat Robertson on the 700 Club explained this well. He said if your spouse is cruel/abusive, does not seek counseling, or after counseling continues in the abusive/cruel behavior, the spouse has left, in a spiritual sense, already. He called divorce, in this case, the Pauline privilege. Extreme cruelty and abuse are valid reasons for divorce. I do not say to leave a marriage without much prayer, godly counseling, and thought about the cost to you and your family for such a decision. It rips apart you, your spouse and your children, physically, spiritually, and emotionally. God does hate divorce, but in my estimation, allows it in cases of extreme cruelty and abuse, and if there is a clear and certain perception that the spouse is not going to change. Ultimately, such a decision is between you and God.

Here are other scriptures on cruelty, roughness, harshness:

"And Joseph saw his brethren, and he knew them, but made himself strange unto them, and spake roughly unto them; and he said unto them, whence come ye? And they said, from the land of Canaan to buy food." (Genesis 42:7)

"So Jonathan made a covenant with the house of David, saying, Let the LORD even require it at the hand of David's enemies." (1 Samuel 20:16)

"And the king answered the people roughly, and forsook the old men's counsel that they gave him." (1 Kings 12:13)

Desire

Desire: An emotion or excitement of the mind, directed to the attainment or possession of an object from which pleasure, sensual, intellectual or spiritual is expected; a passion excited by the love of an object, or uneasiness at want of it, and directed to its attainment or possession. Desire is a wish to possess some gratification or source of happiness which is supposed to be obtainable. Desire when directed solely to sensual enjoyment differs little from appetite.

Satisfaction: That state of mind which results from the gratification of desire; repose of mind or contentment with present possession and enjoyment.

Fulfillment: Accomplishment; completion; Execution; performance.

Envy: To feel uneasiness, mortification or discontent at the sight of superior excellence, reputation or happiness enjoyed by another; To repine at another's prosperity, to grieve one's self at the real or supposed superiority of another and to hate him on that account.

Comment: Socialism is a form of envy. Those with less desire the riches of those with more (wanting redistribution of wealth).

"Delight thyself also in the Lord: and he shall give thee the desires of thine heart." (Psalm 37:4)

"He will fulfil the desire of them that fear him: he also will hear their cry, and will save them." (Psalm 145:19)

"For God hath put in their hearts to fulfil his will, and to agree, and give their kingdom unto the beast, until the words of God shall be fulfilled." (Revelation 17:17)

"For we ourselves also were sometimes foolish, disobedient, deceived, serving divers lusts and pleasures, living in malice and envy, hateful, and hating one another." (Titus 3:3)

It was my heart's desire to be healed of my bipolar illness and not be dependent on medication. On a number of occasions I went to the church altar, and asked the elders to pray for me and anoint me with oil. After three years, my doctor began to carefully take me off my medication. But it wasn't meant to be. The word of God and prayer were not enough. God wanted me to continue to take my medication. God healed me through the word of God, prayer, godly doctors, and medicine. I know now I can't go off my medication.

There is hope for the mentally ill. Mental illness is a difficult illness to cure by man's standards, because of the complexity of the mind and our emotions. There is hope, however. I believe there are men who are doing their best to understand these complexities and to help those who are ill. I applaud these efforts by psychiatrists and psychologists. Unfortunately, I believe these efforts will fail without the wisdom of the Scripture and a prayerful and intimate relationship with God by the patient.

A number of studies point to the fact that faith in God has a positive effect on the soul and heart of man. My godly Christian counselor said this when he began my counseling, "My counseling will be based on sound psychological studies and the word of God." His counseling and the medication set me free of my illness. The flexibility regarding my medication by the psychiatrist was also helpful. His reasonableness helped to build my trust in him. I could also sense a compassion in him; he wanted to help me. I am grateful for both.

Other scriptures on desire:

"Brethren, my heart's desire and prayer to God for Israel is, that they might be saved." (Romans 10:1)

"Follow after charity, and desire spiritual gifts, but rather that ye may prophesy." (1 Corinthians 14:1)

"But now they desire a better country, that is, an heavenly: wherefore God is not ashamed to be called their God: for he hath prepared for them a city." (Hebrews 11:16)

Despair

Despair: Hopelessness, a hopeless state; a destitution of hope or expectation. Loss of hope in the mercy of God.

> "Therefore I hated life; because the work that is wrought under the sun is grievous unto me: for all is vanity and vexation of spirit. Yea, I hated all my labour which I had taken under the sun: because I should leave it unto the man that shall be after me. And who knoweth whether he shall be a wise man or a fool? yet shall he have rule over all my labour wherein I have laboured, and wherein I have shewed myself wise under the sun. This is also vanity. Therefore I went about to cause my heart to despair of all the labour which I took under the sun." (Ecclesiastes 2:17-20)

I have felt despair. There was a time when every decision I made seemed to end up wrong. My prayers for wisdom were not being answered and I wasn't sure where to turn. I believe at this time God hid his face from me for a short time as it says in Psalm 30:6-7, "And in my prosperity I said, I shall never be moved. Lord, by thy favour thou hast made my mountain to stand strong: thou didst hide thy face, and I was troubled."

The worst time in my life when I believe God hid himself from me was during my breakdown and thereafter. The pearl that resulted, however, was my salvation. During this time, my prayers weren't being answered, but my wife offered her help and advice, and I felt I was back on track again. Sometimes, all it takes to lift a person from despair is a small amount of support, kindness and understanding. I was very grateful to my wife. Yes, everything did seem to be vanity (meaningless), but a helping hand lifted me up. Beyond that, I learned I was trying to control my circumstances through prayer. I was not in control even through prayer; God was.

I had to accept that if God didn't want to change my circumstances, I would have to accept God's will for my life. The Serenity Prayer says, "God grant me the serenity to accept the things I cannot change, the courage to change the things I can, and the wisdom to know the difference." Living one day at a time, enjoying one moment at a time, accepting hardships as a pathway to peace, taking them as Jesus did, trusting that you will make things alright if I surrender to His will. I make this daily and conscious commitment so that I may be reasonably happy in this life and superbly happy in the next.

Other scriptures on despair:

"For we would not, brethren, have you ignorant of our trouble which came to us in Asia, that we were pressed out of measure, above strength, insomuch that we despaired even of life: But we had the sentence of death in ourselves, that we should not trust in ourselves, but in God which raiseth the dead:" (2 Corinthians 1:8-9)

"We are troubled on every side, yet not distressed; we are perplexed, but not in despair; Persecuted, but not forsaken; cast down, but not destroyed;" (2 Corinthians 4:8-9)

Disappoint

Disappoint: The defeat of expectation, wish, hope, desire or intention; to frustrate; to balk; to hinder from the possession or enjoyment of that which was intended, desired, hoped or expected. We say a man is disappointed of his hopes or expectations, or his hopes, desires, intentions or expectations are disappointed.

Hinder: To stop; interrupt or obstruct; to impede; or prevent from moving forward by any means.

> "Without counsel purposes are disappointed: but in the multitude of counsellors they are established." (Proverbs 15:22)

> "Ye did run well; who did hinder you that ye should not obey the truth? This persuasion cometh not of him that calleth you. A little leaven leaveneth the whole lump." (Galatians 5:7-9)

> "Likewise, ye husbands, dwell with them according to knowledge, giving honour unto the wife, as unto the weaker vessel, and as being heirs together of the grace of life; that your prayers be not hindered." (1 Peter 3:7)

I have been disappointed on a large level. My dreams for helping others based on the vision God has given me don't seem to be shared by my wife and she seems even to be opposed. What a disappointment to me. My dream was to help others with similar problems as myself. My dream was that my wife would share in this godly purpose. When dreams are shattered, there is disappointment. My dream gives me purpose, hope for the future.

Beyond this, why are our prayers disappointed or hindered? Prayers can be hindered or disappointed for several reasons. With anything we can also go overboard and seek too much counsel and too often. The small things can be decided for yourself.

Satan and his minions (wicked angels or people) can also hinder your efforts (Galatians 5:7-9). Daniel 10:12-13 says,

"Then said he unto me, Fear not, Daniel: for from the first day that thou didst set thine heart to understand, and to chasten thyself before thy God, thy words were heard, and I am come for thy words. But the prince of the kingdom of Persia withstood me one and twenty days: but, lo, Michael, one of the chief princes, came to help me; and I remained there with the kings of Persia."

Daniel's prayers were hindered by a fallen angel, one of great power. Only Michael, the most powerful angel, was able to free up the other angel to answer Daniel's prayers.

Acts 8:36 indicates that we must believe with all our hearts and it will happen. In Mark 11:23-26, it says something very similar:

"For verily I say unto you, That whosoever shall say unto this mountain, Be thou removed, and be thou cast into the sea; and shall not doubt in his heart, but shall believe that those things which he saith shall come to pass; he shall have whatsoever he saith. Therefore I say unto you, What things soever ye desire, when ye pray, believe that ye receive them, and ye shall have them. And when ye stand praying, forgive, if ye have ought against any: that your Father also which is in heaven may forgive you your trespasses. But if ye do not forgive, neither will your Father which is in heaven forgive your trespasses."

Two important hindrances are doubt and lack of forgiveness. If we doubt that our prayers will be answered, they won't be. I have had prayers that have seemed not to be answered but it was a matter of timing. We need to stand firm and not doubt.

It may seem unbearable but God will not give us more than we can bear. Also, if we don't forgive those who have offended or wronged us, this too will hinder our prayers.

More scripture on disappointment or hindrances:

"And as they went on their way, they came unto a certain water: and the eunuch said, See, here is water; what doth hinder me to be baptized?" (Acts 8:36)

Fear

Fear: A feeling of anxiety caused by the presence or nearness of danger, evil or pain. Prolonged fear is the absence of faith or trust in God.

Anxiety: A state of being uneasy, apprehensive, or worried about what may happen; concern about a future event.

Worry: To feel troubled, uneasy or distressed.

"A prudent man foreseeth the evil, and hideth himself: but the simple pass on, and are punished." (Proverbs 22:3)

"Be careful for nothing; but in every thing by prayer and supplication with thanksgiving let your requests be made known unto God. And the peace of God, which passeth all understanding, shall keep your hearts and minds through Christ Jesus." (Philippians 4:6-7)

"Have not I commanded thee? Be strong and of a good courage; be not afraid, neither be thou dismayed: for the LORD thy God is with thee whithersoever thou goest." (Joshua 1:9)

Fear can either be normal or abnormal. By this I mean, normal fear is when we confront danger, evil, or pain. When we keep a prolonged fear and repeat it over and over in our hearts, this is abnormal and may be called paranoia or a phobia. Whenever I begin to worry or be fearful, I immediately go to prayer. I think on God's omnipotent power and that if he chooses, he can protect us from anything. This employs a great trust in our creator and protector. Psalm 91 is a great prayer of protection which the military has often used.

Other scriptures on fear/worry/anxiety:

"Take therefore no thought for the morrow: for the morrow shall take thought for the things of itself. Sufficient unto the day is the evil thereof." (Matthew 6:34)

"For God hath not given us the spirit of fear; but of power, and of love, and of a sound mind." (2 Timothy 1:7)

"So that we may boldly say, The Lord is my helper, and I will not fear what man shall do unto me." (Hebrews 13:6)

Fulfilled

Fulfilled: Completed.

Fullness: The state of being filled, so as to leave no part vacant. The state of abounding or being in great plenty; abundance, completeness; the state of a thing in which nothing is wanted; perfection.

Whole: Complete; entire; not defective or imperfect; unimpaired; unbroken; uninjured; sound; not hurt or sick.

Perfect: Complete.

> "Thou preparest a table before me in the presence of mine enemies: thou anointest my head with oil; my cup runneth over." (Psalm 23:5)

> "The thief cometh not, but for to steal, and to kill, and to destroy: I am come that they might have life, and that they might have it more abundantly." (John 10:10)

Prior to my breakdown, everything seemed fine. I had good parents who cared about me. I did OK in school and I had a lot of friends. But something was missing in my life. I was unsaved and my heart was not complete, full, or whole. There are many ways God makes us feel complete, fulfilled, or whole. He can fill us with blessings. Malachi 3:10 says, "Bring ye all the tithes into the storehouse, that there may be meat in mine house and prove me now herewith, saith the Lord of hosts, if I will not open you the windows of heaven, and pour out a blessing, that there shall not be room enough to receive it." Is this a financial blessing? Perhaps, but God blesses us in so many ways.

> "Therefore take no thought, saying, 'What shall we eat?' or, 'What shall we drink?' or, 'Wherewithal shall we be clothed?' (For after all these things do the Gentiles seek:)

for your heavenly Father knoweth that ye have need of all these things. But seek ye first the kingdom of God, and his righteousness; and all these things shall be added unto you." (Matthew 6:31-33)

When we fall away from a close relationship with God for whatever reason, I believe that God sometimes causes us to lack in finances so as to draw us back to Him. There is nothing more important than our relationship with God; seeking him in His word; praying; worshipping Him; honoring and serving Him in every aspect of our life, by our work ethic, by the things we bring before our eyes, by the love and respect we show to our families and others. The list could go on and on.

A few more scriptures on fulfillment:

"If ye keep my commandments, ye shall abide in my love; even as I have kept my Father's commandments, and abide in his love. These things have I spoken unto you, that my joy might remain in you, and that your joy might be full." (John 15:10-11)

"And to know the love of Christ, which passeth knowledge, that ye might be filled with all the fullness of God." (Ephesians 3:19)

Greed

Greediness: Ardent desire.

Greedy: Having a keen desire of anything; eager to obtain; as greedy of gain.

> "He that is greedy of gain troubleth his own house; but he that hateth gifts shall live." (Proverbs 15:27)

There is no rest in greed. A greedy person, if left unchecked, desires more and more and is never satisfied with the possessions he/she has and eventually loses their thankfulness for what they do have. Some people call a child spoiled when he/she complains and throws a fit when they can't have a toy in the store. More appropriately this is an act of greed. My wife and I have to be careful with our children, as we both have a giving heart. An episode of the Veggie Tales show, titled Madame Blueberry, addresses this subject well. Madame Blueberry wanted more and more things until her tree house was so full of things that the house toppled over. Madame Blueberry learned to be thankful and content with what she had, and not want more. The video is excellent and may be helpful to help curb your child's feelings in this area.

Some more helpful scripture on greed:

> "And they lay wait for their own blood; they lurk privily for their own lives. So are the ways of every one that is greedy of gain; which taketh away the life of the owners thereof." (Proverbs 1:18-19)

> "A bishop then must be blameless, the husband of one wife, vigilant, sober, of good behaviour, given to hospitality, apt to teach; Not given to wine, no striker, not greedy of filthy lucre; but patient, not a brawler, not covetous;" (1 Timothy 3:2-3)

Guilty

Guilt: Feelings of guilt may range from shame; wanting to conceal it, fearfulness, remorse, conviction and finally, a hardened heart.

Conviction: The act of convincing or compelling one to admit the truth of a charge; the act of convincing of sin or sinfulness; the state of being convinced or convicted by conscience; the state of being sensible of guilt; as the convictions of a sinner may be temporary or lasting and efficacious. By conviction a sinner is brought to repentance. Men often sin against the conviction of their own consciences.

Harden: To confirm in wickedness; opposition or enmity; to make obdurate (hardened against good or favor); to make insensible or unfeeling; as to harden one against impressions of pity or tenderness.

Remorse: The keen pain or anguish excited by a sense of guilt; compunction of conscience for a crime committed.

> "Wherefore then do ye harden your hearts, as the Egyptians and Pharaoh hardened their hearts? when he had wrought wonderfully among them, did they not let the people go, and they departed?" (1 Samuel 6:6)

> "For mine iniquities are gone over mine head: as an heavy burden they are too heavy for me." (Psalm 38:4)

God is said to harden the heart when He withdraws the influence of His spirit from men, leaving them to pursue their own corrupt inclinations. Conviction causes unrest. The Holy Spirit convicts. The conviction of our sin burdens our soul. It may bring a soul to repentance or cause it to draw closer and closer to that hardened state of the heart. Sin can bring misery and sin can cause fear or terror in the heart. You can overcome the feeling of guilt by forgiving yourself and not committing a sin again.

Other scriptures on guilt or conviction:

"For I acknowledge my transgressions: and my sin *is* ever before me." (Psalm 51:3)

"Brethren, I count not myself to have apprehended: but this one thing I do, forgetting those things which are behind, and reaching forth unto those things which are before, I press toward the mark for the prize of the high calling of God in Christ Jesus." (Philippians 3:13,14)

Hard Heartedness

Hard Hearted: Cruel; pitiless; merciless; unfeeling; inhuman; inexorable; (noun, Hard Heartedness): Want (void) of feeling or tenderness; cruelty; inhumanity.

"And the LORD said unto Moses, When thou goest to return into Egypt, see that thou do all those wonders before Pharaoh, which I have put in thine hand: but I will harden his heart, that he shall not let the people go." (Exodus 4:21)

"And when he had looked round about on them with anger, being grieved for the hardness of their hearts, he saith unto the man, Stretch forth thine hand. And he stretched it out: and his hand was restored whole as the other." (Mark 3:5)

"But the house of Israel will not hearken unto thee; for they will not hearken unto me: for all the house of Israel are impudent and hardhearted." (Ezekiel 3:7)

Emotions are like the rudder, steering the ship through the relational waters. The man steering is like the mind. But without the word of God he would surely steer a crooked course in relationships with other men and women. Don't ever take for granted the emotions/mind God has given us. We should have a deep appreciation for them. There is a beauty in our emotions/mind. There is purpose in our emotions. To love, to have joy, to hope; these are all beautiful emotions. To think clearly is a great gift. When you can't feel these emotions, or think to your full potential, it is a terrible thing.

I, personally, have been placed on medications that nullified or voided many of my emotions. Being over-medicated also dulled my thinking. God created us in a wonderful way. Be thankful for the way God made you. Don't take for granted what someday may be taken away from you. I pray no one experiences the terrible feeling of a hardened heart. Come to Christ while it is still possible.

As seen in Exodus 4:21, God hardened the heart of Pharaoh. God allowed my heart to be hardened by over-medication so I could describe how it felt. I was unfeeling, almost inhuman, pitiless, and merciless, much like a hardened convict with a seared conscience. Yet, the only thing that kept me from accepting all these feelings or lack of feelings was what I knew to be right and wrong from the Bible. I knew to do acts of kindness, to have mercy, to show pity – even though I didn't feel like it. My mind kept me on track when the rudder of my feelings had been lost or damaged. I consider the medication I was on to be very dangerous at the wrong dosage. It has the potential to cause a person to be cruel and inhuman. I implore all to turn to God, so as not to have their heart hardened by God or Satan.

Other scriptures on the hardened heart:

"He hath blinded their eyes, and hardened their heart; that they should not see with their eyes, nor understand with their heart, and be converted, and I should heal them." (John 12:40)

"For the scripture saith unto Pharaoh, Even for this same purpose have I raised thee up, that I might shew my power in thee, and that my name might be declared throughout all the earth. Therefore hath he mercy on whom he will have mercy, and whom he will he hardeneth." (Romans 9:17-18)

Hate

Hate: To dislike greatly; to have a great aversion to. It expresses less than abhor, detest, and abominate, unless pronounced with a peculiar emphasis.

Bitterness: Extreme enmity; grudge; hatred; an excessive degree of implacableness of passions and emotions as the bitterness of anger.

Enmity: The quality of being an enemy, the opposite of friendship; ill will; hatred; unfriendly dispositions; malevolence. A malevolent heart rejoices in the misfortunes of others.

> "Ye have heard that it hath been said, Thou shalt love thy neighbour, and hate thine enemy. But I say unto you, Love your enemies, bless them that curse you, do good to them that hate you, and pray for them which despitefully use you, and persecute you;" (Matthew 5:43- 44)

> "Ye that love the LORD, hate evil: he preserveth the souls of his saints; he delivereth them out of the hand of the wicked." (Psalm 97:10)

> "These six things doth the LORD hate: yea, seven are an abomination unto him: A proud look, a lying tongue, and hands that shed innocent blood, An heart that deviseth wicked imaginations, feet that be swift in running to mischief, A false witness that speaketh lies, and he that soweth discord among brethren." (Proverbs 6:16-19)

It's been said many times that many political insiders hate President Trump. I believe this to be so. Every good thing the President tries to do, the politicians obstruct or hinder him. Despite their hindrances, President Trump has had some great successes. He stands against the shedding of innocent blood; murder committed by immigrants, or shedding of innocent unborn lives. He is trying his best to protect us from the drugs pouring over our southern border, and is working toward peace with North Korea. In all of these situations both the majority of the media and the politicians have opposed him. My comment to the media and the politicians is found in Isaiah 5:20, "Woe unto them that call evil good and good evil, put darkness for light and light for darkness, put bitter for sweet and sweet for bitterness." "There is a way that seemeth right unto a man but the end thereof is destruction" (Proverbs 14:12). This is the path most of the media have taken as well as the majority of politicians.

Other scriptures on hate:

"The fear of the LORD is to hate evil: pride, and arrogancy, and the evil way, and the froward mouth, do I hate." (Proverbs 8:13)

"Thou shalt not hate thy brother in thine heart: thou shalt in any wise rebuke thy neighbour, and not suffer sin upon him." (Leviticus 19:17)

Comment: Rebuke is defined as to chide, chasten or correct. It is better to rebuke your brother if it bothers you too much, than to hold hate in your heart. But mostly, we should show love, mercy, and kindness to those who offend us.

Hope

Hope: Expectation of a favorable outcome.

Expectation: A looking forward to something with a fore-taste of the pleasure or distress it causes.

> "Now faith is the substance of things hoped for, the evidence of things not seen." (Hebrews 11:1)

> "And now abideth faith, hope, charity, these three; but the greatest of these is charity." (1 Corinthians 13:13)

> "That being justified by his grace, we should be made heirs according to the hope of eternal life." (Titus 3:7)

> "Hope deferred maketh the heart sick: but when the desire cometh, it is a tree of life." (Proverbs 13:12)

I would like to start with three quotes from Billy Graham's magazine, "Decision"[2], from an article entitled "New York a Place of Hope."

> "I see God redeeming this pit. We have the god of hope who is sovereign over all. He was in charge before 9/11 and is in charge still. That's the reason we can see his glory at the bottom of this pit" (Major George Polarek, Salvation Army).

> "At the pile I was constantly looking up and seeing the beams: What was in the beam work but crosses! Jesus Christ was right there, just as he was on Calvary. That's the beginning. That's the hope. That's the kingdom" (Michael Anson, Senior, Firefighter and Secretary of Firefighters for Christ).

> "Soaring to me is just putting one foot in front of the other. I wonder how will I go on with everything. But God gets

---

2 "New York: A Place of Hope". *Decision*, Sept. 2002.

me up in the morning and I realize these days have their purpose. I cling to Psalm 68:5, "A father of the fatherless, and a judge of the widows, is God in his holy habitation" (Lori Crotty, widow and mother of three).

There is a constant war by the world, the devil, and his followers against our emotions. The word can fortify us emotionally. 2 Corinthians 10:4-6 says,

"(For the weapons of our warfare are not carnal, but mighty through God to the pulling down of strong holds;) Casting down imaginations, and every high thing that exalteth itself against the knowledge of God, and bringing into captivity every thought to the obedience of Christ; And having in a readiness to revenge all disobedience, when your obedience is fulfilled."

The hardness of the way can cause us to lose hope or be discouraged. Exodus 1:14 says, "And they (the Egyptians) made their lives bitter with hard bondage in mortar and in brick and in all manner of service in the field: all their service, wherein they made them serve, was with rigour." The Egyptian people so burdened the Israelis, that they sometimes became discouraged and I'm sure felt hopeless. The hardness of the way is sometimes extremely tough and almost brings us to the breaking point.

The story of Exodus is a story of hopelessness, yet also a story of hope: the hope that God would deliver them. Through Moses, God worked mighty miracles. Their faith maintained their hope, until God sent them their deliverer. I find great hope in the story of Exodus. God can deliver us from our troubles and burdens if we are faithful to Him. Daniel 3:17-18 says, "If it be so, our God is able to deliver us from the fiery furnace and he will deliver us out of thine hand O king, but if not, be it known unto thee, O king, that we will not serve thy gods, nor worship the golden image which thou hast set up."

Loneliness

Loneliness: Solitude; retirement; seclusion from company.

Alone: Single; solitary; without the presence of another; separately; by itself.

"And the LORD God said, It is not good that the man should be alone; I will make him an help meet for him." (Genesis 2:18)

"He sitteth alone and keepeth silence, because he hath borne it upon him." (Lamentations 3:28)

"Then cometh Jesus with them unto a place called Gethsemane, and saith unto the disciples, Sit ye here, while I go and pray yonder. And he took with him Peter and the two sons of Zebedee, and began to be sorrowful and very heavy. Then saith he unto them, My soul is exceeding sorrowful, even unto death: tarry ye here, and watch with me. And he went a little further, and fell on his face, and prayed, saying, O my Father, if it be possible, let this cup pass from me: nevertheless not as I will, but as thou wilt. And he cometh unto the disciples, and findeth them asleep, and saith unto Peter, What, could ye not watch with me one hour?" (Matthew 26: 36-40)

There was a time in my life when I didn't have a personal relationship with God. I had a breakdown and felt everyone had abandoned me. I felt so alone and I believe it is the worst feeling anyone can endure. Although we cannot fully experience what Christ felt on the cross, I believe what I experienced was much like what Christ felt, i.e. separation from God and man. He was rejected by God and man when he took on all our sins. Because of this, He felt separated from God, and said, "My God, my God, why hast thou forsaken me?" (Matthew 27:46, Mark 13:14, Psalm 22:1) Can you sense the loneliness he felt when he spoke those words? God's word says we will be eternally separated from God if we don't come to have a relationship with Him. Specifically, in Matthew 25:32-46, it says:

"And before him shall be gathered all nations: and he shall separate them one from another, as a shepherd divideth his sheep from the goats: And he shall set the sheep on his right hand, but the goats on the left. Then shall the King say unto them on his right hand, Come, ye blessed of my Father, inherit the kingdom prepared for you from the foundation of the world: For I was an hungred, and ye gave me meat: I was thirsty, and ye gave me drink: I was a stranger, and ye took me in: Naked, and ye clothed me: I was sick, and ye visited me: I was in prison, and ye came unto me. Then shall the righteous answer him, saying, Lord, when saw we thee an hungred, and fed thee? or thirsty, and gave thee drink? When saw we thee a stranger, and took thee in? or naked, and clothed thee? Or when saw we thee sick, or in prison, and came unto thee? And the King shall answer and say unto them, Verily I say unto you, Inasmuch as ye have done it unto one of the least of these my brethren, ye have done it unto me. Then shall he say also unto them on the left hand, Depart from me, ye cursed, into everlasting fire, prepared for the devil and his angels: For I was an hungred, and ye gave me no meat: I was thirsty, and ye gave me no drink: I was a stranger, and ye took me not in: naked, and ye clothed me not: sick, and in prison, and ye visited me not. Then shall they also answer him, saying, Lord, when saw we thee an hungred, or athirst, or a stranger, or naked, or sick, or in prison, and did not minister unto thee? Then shall he answer them, saying, Verily I say unto you, Inasmuch as ye did it not to one of the least of these, ye did it not to me. And these shall go away into everlasting punishment: but the righteous into life eternal."

Relationships with people can ease the emptiness we feel, when we don't have a relationship with God, but can never fill the hole. If you are really lonely, I encourage you to develop a relationship with God through prayer, worship, and studying his word. I also encourage you to develop relationships with other Christians. Ask God to give you the wisdom on how to do that.

Another scripture on overcoming loneliness:

"Who shall separate us from the love of Christ? Shall tribulation, or distress, or persecution, or famine, or nakedness, or peril, or sword?" (Romans 8:35)

Lust

Lust: Longing desire; eagerness to possess or enjoy; as the lust of gain; to have carnal desire; to desire eagerly the gratification of carnal appetite.

Carnal: Given to sensual indulgence; flesh, fleshly; sensual.

"But I say unto you, that whosoever looketh on a woman to lust after her hath committed adultery with her already in his heart." (Matthew 5:28)

My wife was divorced when I married her – God hates divorce and some would say that it is a sin. I believe God hates (greatly dislikes) divorce because of how it hurts the families that are torn apart emotionally, spiritually, financially, etc. My wife was divorced due to the adultery of her ex-husband. For her ex-husband, the adultery he committed started with feelings of lust in his heart. He had become deeply involved in pornography and hid it from her for some time. He visited massage parlors for sexual reasons.

Deceit by her ex-husband was not uncommon. When he was found out, he cried for some time and said he would mend his ways before a pastor. Although, his behavior continued. He professed to be a Christian and worshipped with the best of them prior to their marriage. People change. Why would he continue in this behavior and put their marriage at risk?

Pornography had created such a strong feeling of lust in this man and he couldn't set himself free, and perhaps didn't want to. Sin is enjoyable for a season until reality sets in. He was addicted to sex and it all started as it says in Matthew 5:28, he looked on a woman to lust after her. The results of his lust were very destructive. He not only harmed my wife emotionally but tore apart the union which God had intended between her and him.

"Flee fornication. Every sin that a man doeth is without the body; but he that committeth fornication sinneth against his own body." (1 Corinthians 6:18)

Fornication is defined as the incontinence or lewdness of the unmarried (including premarital intercourse); adultery; incest; idolatry; a forsaking of the true God and worshipping idols. Flee from, avoid potentially lustful situations and places such as bars, drinking establishments. Another way to avoid lust is if you see a man/woman who is attractive to you, you may want to avoid contact with that person. If that is not possible, call on God to help you avoid any lustful feelings or situations. Another way is to redirect your thoughts to your wife/husband and the times you have been satisfied by him/her on all levels, including sex. Christians often have beauty in their countenance because of Christ that shines through them. My thoughts for these people are that they will make a wonderful spouse for some other Christian and then I turn my thoughts elsewhere.

Other scriptures on lust:

"But my people would not hearken to my voice; and Israel would none of me. So I gave them up unto their own hearts' lust: and they walked in their own counsels." (Psalm 81:11-12)

"And likewise also the men, leaving the natural use of the woman, burned in their lust one toward another; men with men working that which is unseemly, and receiving in themselves that recompence of their error which was meet." (Romans 1:27)

Pleasure

Pleasure: Gratification of the senses or of the mind; agreeable sensations or emotions; the excitement, relish or happiness produced by the enjoyment or the expectation of good; opposed to pain. We receive pleasure from the indulgence of appetite; from the view of a beautiful landscape; from the harmony of sounds; from agreeable society; from the expectation of seeing an absent friend. Pleasure, bodily, and mental, carnal and spiritual, constitutes the whole of positive happiness, as pain constitutes the whole of misery.

Delight: To affect with great pleasure; to please highly; to give or afford high satisfaction or joy; as a beautiful landscape delights the eye; harmony delights the ear; the good conduct of children, and especially their piety, delights their parents.

"I said in mine heart, Go to now, I will prove thee with mirth, therefore enjoy pleasure: and, behold, this also is vanity." (Ecclesiastes 2:1)

"I will delight myself in thy statutes: I will not forget thy word." (Psalm 119:16)

"Yet they seek me daily, and delight to know my ways, as a nation that did righteousness, and forsook not the ordinance of their God: they ask of me the ordinances of justice; they take delight in approaching to God." (Isaiah 58:2)

The theme of Ecclesiastes is that everything, everything is meaningless without God. Solomon spoke of the pleasures of great works such as building houses, planting vineyards, gardens, orchards; having servants and maidens; possessions of great and small cattle. Yet, Solomon states twenty-three times in Ecclesiastes that these are all meaningless. In the end he realizes they are meaningless without God.

In my own life I have pleasure in observing the beauty of flowers and enjoy watching plants grow, yet my greatest pleasure, my delight, is in God and His word; the wisdom of the Bible; its depth of knowledge and secrets.

Other scriptures on pleasure and delight:

"Make me to go in the path of thy commandments; for therein do I delight." (Psalm 119:35)

"He that loveth pleasure shall be a poor man: he that loveth wine and oil shall not be rich." (Proverbs 21:17)

Shame

Shame: A painful sensation excited by a consciousness of guilt, or having done something which injures the reputation; or by the exposure of that which nature or modesty prompts us to conceal. Shame is particularly excited by the disclosure of actions which, in the view of men, are mean and degrading. Hence, it is often or always manifested by a downcast look or by blushes, called confusion of the face. That which brings reproach and degrades a person in the estimation of others.

"When pride cometh, then cometh shame: but with the lowly is wisdom." (Proverbs 11:2)

"The rod and reproof give wisdom: but a child left to himself bringeth his mother to shame." (Proverbs 29:15)

"Yea, let none that wait on thee be ashamed: let them be ashamed which transgress without cause." (Psalm 25:3)

My wife's heart's desire was, and is, to have a child, but her infertility has not allowed her to have one thus far. She has struggled deeply with this issue. We decided to look into adopting. The more we got into the process, the more they wanted to know about us. I don't believe they left many stones unturned, including my bipolar disorder. For me, being mentally ill caused me to have a deep sense of shame. I felt flawed in the most vital aspect of my being, i.e. my heart or soul. This shame was also caused by the fact that much of the world looks down on the mentally ill. In the world's eyes, I believe that many people feel that the mentally ill are weak-minded or just plain weak.

As they began to ask the questions, a terrible feeling of shame began to develop in me. I struggled with the questions, with the shame, and I believe the adoption process to be the hardest thing I have ever done. I had to go beyond the shame of my mental illness and give my wife her heart's desire.

I believe my wife sensed some of my struggle, but not the severity of it. I overcame my shame, but realized how weak I am as a man without the Lord's help. I had prayed for strength on a number of occasions and I got through it. "I can do all things through Christ which strengtheneth me" (Philippians 4:13). The rewards have been great as a result of this adoption. I love my daughter deeply and she returns that love in ways I could not have imagined. I tell people she makes me feel ten feet tall. With any child comes responsibility to shape their character, and this also was more difficult than I could have imagined.

The first feelings of shame occurred in the Garden of Eden. In Genesis 3:8-10 it says,

> "And they heard the voice of the Lord God walking in the garden in the cool of the day: and Adam and his wife hid themselves from the presence of the Lord God amongst the trees of the garden. And the Lord God called unto Adam, and said unto him, Where art thou? And he said, I heard thy voice in the garden, and I was afraid, because I was naked; and I hid myself."

Don't our souls feel naked and of terrible weakness when we have sinned and it's revealed? Adam and Eve tried to conceal themselves and their sin from God. They felt afraid, guilty, and ashamed because they had done wrong in God's eyes. Their hearts and their character had become deeply flawed because they transgressed God's law. How weak they were, and how weak we all are without God.

I became saved in 1991 and the road to recovery has been both exciting and joyful for me. Although I felt deep shame during the adoption process, I have gotten closer to God and feelings of joy and peace have begun to flood my heart. God is bringing back the joy in my life, and "the joy of the Lord is my strength" (Nehemiah 8:10).

Other scriptures on shame:

> "O LORD, the hope of Israel, all that forsake thee shall be ashamed, and they that depart from me shall be written in

the earth, because they have forsaken the LORD, the fountain of living waters." (Jeremiah 17:13)

"Let the proud be ashamed; for they dealt perversely with me without a cause: but I will meditate in thy precepts." (Psalm 119:78)

"And said, O my God, I am ashamed and blush to lift up my face to thee, my God: for our iniquities are increased over our head, and our trespass is grown up unto the heavens." (Ezra 9:6)

Sorrow

Sorrow: The uneasiness or pain of mind which is produced by the loss of any good, or of frustrated hopes of good or expected loss of happiness; to be sad.

Grief: The pain of mind produced by loss, misfortune, injury or evils of any kind; sorrow; regret. We experience grief when we lose a friend, when we incur loss, when we consider ourselves injured.

Weep: To express sorrow; grief or anguish by outcry. To express grief by crying out or shedding of tears.

> "For his anger endureth but a moment; in his favour is life: weeping may endure for a night, but joy cometh in the morning." (Psalm 30:5)

I would like to relate an experience I had recently in which I felt a deep sense of grief. My hand was injured and it had become infected. I was convinced I was going to die. My thoughts turned to my adopted daughter who had experienced abandonment by her birth mother. She was left alone in the crib for a long period of time. She had a great fear of being alone or being away from us as parents. How could she handle the loss of her father?

I struggled at what to say to her before I went to the hospital because of the fears she had and I asked God for wisdom. We went out on the porch and I said to her someday daddy may die and go to heaven, but I'll still be here with you. I pointed to my head, the seat of our emotions, the biblical heart. I said even though you may not be able to see daddy, he'll be up here in your heart. I spoke those things and she understood. My daughter is extremely sensitive in this area. After our talk, I took her out to the swing, which she loved dearly, and sang America the Beautiful.

Other scriptures on sorrow, grief and weeping:

"Jesus wept." (John 11:35)

"And God shall wipe away all tears from their eyes; and there shall be no more death, neither sorrow, nor crying, neither shall there be any more pain: for the former things are passed away." (Revelation 21:4)

Sympathy

Sympathize: To have a common feeling; as of bodily pleasure or pain. We sympathize with our friends in distress. We feel some pain when we see them pained, or we are informed of their distress, even at a distance.

Pity: The feeling or suffering of one person, excited by the distresses of another; sympathy with the grief or misery of another; compassion or fellow-suffering.

> "Finally, be ye all of one mind, having compassion one of another, love as brethren, be pitiful, be courteous:" (1 Peter 3:8)

> "He that hath pity upon the poor lendeth unto the LORD; and that which he hath given will he pay him again." (Proverbs 19:17)

> "To him that is afflicted pity should be shewed from his friend; but he forsaketh the fear of the Almighty." (Job 6:14)

My pastor's daughter is in great pain. The pain is so great that she is often in the fetal position. Over two years ago, we were told they had visited twenty-one doctors. They cut some nerves and thought the problem was resolved, but the pain returned worse than ever. The suffering of our pastor's child is ripping at his heart, and wearing him down. From a doctrinal standpoint there seems to be little hope. The pain our pastor is feeling, is pity or sympathy. How terrible he must feel to see his child suffer. Man is limited but with God all things are possible.

Other scriptures on sympathy, pity:

> "Have pity upon me, have pity upon me, O ye my friends; for the hand of God hath touched me." (Job 19:21)

> "Behold, we count them happy which endure. Ye have heard of the patience of Job, and have seen the end of the Lord; that the Lord is very pitiful, and of tender mercy.

Is any sick among you? let him call for the elders of the church; and let them pray over him, anointing him with oil in the name of the Lord: And the prayer of faith shall save the sick, and the Lord shall raise him up; and if he have committed sins, they shall be forgiven him." (James 5:11, 14-15)

Thankfulness

Thankfulness: Expression of gratitude, acknowledgement of a favor. Gratitude; a lively sense of good received.

Gratitude: An emotion of the heart, excited by a favor or benefit received; a sentiment of kindness or good will towards a benefactor; thankfulness. Gratitude is an agreeable emotion, consisting of or accompanied with good will to a benefactor, and a disposition to make a suitable return of benefits or services, or when no return can be made, with a desire to see the benefactor prosperous and happy. Gratitude is a virtue of the highest excellence, as it implies a feeling and generous heart and a proper sense of duty.

> "Giving thanks always for all things unto God and the Father in the name of our Lord Jesus Christ;" (Ephesians 5:20)

> "Now thanks be unto God, which always causeth us to triumph in Christ, and maketh manifest the savour of his knowledge by us in every place." (2 Corinthians 2:14)

I have gratitude for all the good things mentioned in the chapter on goodness. As strange as it may seem to some, I am also grateful for the horror and torment I experienced in my life. How could this be? It is because I see the end God brought in me; my salvation and my intimate relationship with Him. 2 Corinthians 12:9 says, "And he said unto me, My grace is sufficient for thee: for my strength is made perfect in weakness. Most gladly therefore will I rather glory in my infirmities, that the power of Christ may rest upon me." Ephesians 2:8 says, "For by grace are ye saved through faith; and that not of yourselves: it is the gift of God." How can anyone be less than grateful for such a precious gift?

Paul in Corinthians was in prison chains. Yet, in 2 Corinthians 2:14, Paul says, "thanks be to God". In spite of his troubles and bondage, he gave thanks to God which caused him to triumph over the dismal circumstances he was in. The knowledge of Christ he shared with the prison guards was a sweet aroma to them. In the midst of the dark dingy prison, while in chains, he could see the opportunity to witness to the guards for their salvation.

I am also grateful because I appreciate life so much more. For those who support euthanasia or assisted suicide to alleviate suffering, you are wrong.

Wonder

Wonder: The emotion which is excited by novelty, or presentation to the sight or mind, of something new, unusual, strange, great, extraordinary or not well understood; something that arrests the attention by its novelty, grandeur or inexplicableness. Wonder expresses less than astonishment and much less than amazement.

Wonderful: Adapted to excite wonder or admiration; exciting surprise; strange; astonishing.

Wonderfully: In a manner to excite wonder or surprise.

"And the angel said unto them, Fear not: for, behold, I bring you good tidings of great joy, which shall be to all people. For unto you is born this day in the city of David a Saviour, which is Christ the Lord. And this shall be a sign unto you; Ye shall find the babe wrapped in swaddling clothes, lying in a manger. And suddenly there was with the angel a multitude of the heavenly host praising God, and saying, Glory to God in the highest, and on earth peace, good will toward men. And it came to pass, as the angels were gone away from them into heaven, the shepherds said one to another, Let us now go even unto Bethlehem, and see this thing which is come to pass, which the Lord hath made known unto us. And they came with haste, and found Mary, and Joseph, and the babe lying in a manger. And when they had seen it, they made known abroad the saying which was told them concerning this child. And all they that heard it wondered at those things which were told them by the shepherds." (Luke 2:10-18)

"I will praise thee; for I am fearfully and wonderfully made: marvellous are thy works; and that my soul knoweth right well." (Psalm 139:14)

Christmas is the most wonderful time of year for me. Each year we set out a life-size nativity scene in our front yard. It brings me such joy and wonder. My wife created a crèche and helped build it, which brought her great joy and wonder also. In this busy time of year, it is important not to lose the wonder of Christmas, the wonderful birth of our Lord Jesus Christ. In an ever-darkening world, the joy and light of Christmas continues to shine, despite attempts to blot it out. I encourage you to go out, sing Christmas carols, sing joy unto our Lord and Savior Jesus Christ. Be full of joy on this wonderful time of year! The song has it right, "It's the most wonderful time of the year..."

I think on how we are fearfully and wonderfully made as human beings, created in God's image. I think of the biblical human heart, and how intricate our minds, our emotions and our spirits are. I think back on the birth of my children and the wonder I felt when they were born. No one should ever blot out, destroy, and abort a life so fearfully and wonderfully made. At the end of this chapter, I have enclosed a picture/article that should help you experience the wonder of a child still in the womb about to be born.

Other scriptures on wonder:

"And he began to say unto them, This day is this scripture fulfilled in your ears. And all bare him witness, and wondered at the gracious words which proceeded out of his mouth. And they said, Is not this Joseph's son?" (Luke 4:21-22)

"And they shall be upon thee for a sign and for a wonder, and upon thy seed for ever." (Deuteronomy 28:46)

"Seek the LORD, and his strength: seek his face evermore. Remember his marvellous works that he hath done; his wonders, and the judgments of his mouth;" (Psalm 105:4-5)

Family News From Dr. James Dobson

January 2004

Dear Friends:

It's January, and that means it is time to observe Sanctity of Human Life Month. At the outset, however, I would like to hearken back to the April 2000 edition of *Family News*, in which I shared the remarkable story of Samuel Alexander Armas, a tiny baby boy who, at 21 weeks' gestation, underwent spinal surgery while he was still in his mother's womb.[1] A photographer named Michael Clancy was on hand for the procedure and captured a powerful and heart-wrenching image of Samuel's hand extending from the womb and grasping the finger of the surgeon. This dramatic photograph should have been seen by people around the world, because it illustrates the marvelous humanness of a preborn child. Unfortunately, most of the major news outlets refused to share it with the public.

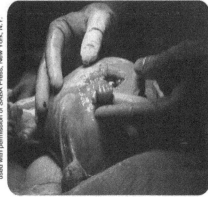

Michael Clancy Photograph of Samuel Alexander Armas used with permission of SABA Press, New York, N.Y.

Given their pro-abortion bias, it isn't difficult to figure out why.

Seeing this wonderful photo reminds me of the struggle to outlaw partial-birth abortion and the many emotional debates surrounding it in the U.S. Congress. Sen. Rick Santorum (R-PA), the most articulate defender of life in the Senate, pleaded repeatedly with his colleagues to end the grotesque procedure by which the brains of un-anaesthetized babies are suctioned out in the final moments of delivery. For eight years, the battle raged.

Coming from the other end of the universe, Sen. Barbara Boxer (D-CA), fought year after year to preserve the legality of partial-birth abortion. For her, killing babies was "a women's health issue" that disregarded entirely the welfare of the child.

In 1999, after President Bill Clinton had shamelessly vetoed a bill banning the procedure in both 1996 and 1997, a new attempt to pass the legislation pitted the two senators in another confrontation. Boxer claimed that partial-birth abortion was medically necessary to save the life of the mother, even though the American Medical Association insisted that it is <u>never needed for that or any other purpose</u>.[2] During the heat of the debate, Santorum asked Boxer, "[Do] you agree, once the child is born, [and] separated from the mother, that the child is protected by the Constitution and cannot be killed[?] Do you agree with that?"[3] Boxer's answer was stunning. "I think that when you bring your baby home, when your baby is born...the baby belongs to your family and has rights," she sputtered.[4] Think for a moment about that disturbing statement that is now immortalized in the Congressional Record. Though she did not say so, the position taken by Sen. Boxer would clearly support the murder of an infant until, and if, the mother and father decide that they want to keep it. As long as the baby is still in the hospital, however, he or she has no rights whatsoever—not even the right not to be killed. This is a tragic example of postmodern reasoning that, if enacted into law, would lead ultimately to infanticide at the whim of the parents.

At this point in the debate, Senator Boxer apparently realized that she had gotten herself in an impossible bind. She shot back at Santorum that she didn't "want to engage in this [type of discussion]."[5] Santorum was persistent. What "if [only] the baby's foot was inside the mother but the rest of the baby was outside, could that baby be

Colorado Springs, CO 80995

---

[3]Dobson, James C. "Family News from Dr. James C. Dobson, PhD." Jan. 2004. Print.

killed?" he asked.[6] She wouldn't answer the question. What "if the baby's toe is inside the mother, you can, in fact, kill that baby?" Santorum pressed.[7] Boxer was breaking and shot back, "absolutely not…I am not answering these questions."[8] Finally, Santorum asked what "if the head is inside the mother, you can kill the baby?"[9] Caught up in her own hypocritical and nonsensical web of logic, Boxer responded by saying that Santorum was "losing his temper."[10] This is how many in the pro-abortion camp deal with these disturbing contradictions—they just ignore them.

The issue of partial-birth abortion was debated one more time in October 2003 when Senators Sam Brownback (R-KS) and Barbara Boxer did battle on the floor of the Senate. During the contentious interchange, Sen. Brownback displayed the historic photo of little Samuel's hand grasping the surgeon's finger, and asked Sen. Boxer if it depicted "the hand of a child" or the hand of a piece of property?[11] Again, Boxer dodged the question awkwardly and replied, "I am not a doctor, and I am not God."[12] Of course, that is exactly what the senator was doing—she was "playing God" with the lives of innocent babies.

For 31 years, the abortion industry has treated preborn babies like non-persons whose lives mean nothing in the eyes of the law. Indeed, the late James McMahon, an early practitioner of the hideous partial-birth abortion procedure, suggested that it isn't a question of *if* a baby is human, but instead, "Who owns the child?"[13]

Well, how about it? Did the perfectly formed little hand in Michael Clancy's photograph belong to a human being, or was it merely part of something the early abortionists used to refer to as "a blob of tissue" or "meaningless protoplasm"? What I am going to share with you now will answer that question for time and eternity. Samuel Alexander Armas, the 21 week-old preborn baby who struggled for life in his mother's uterus, is now the four-year-old, bustling, energetic boy pictured below. What a dramatic testimony this is to the humanity of not only this one child, but every baby conceived down through the ages. Each of us can say with King David, "I praise you because I am fearfully and wonderfully made; your works are wonderful, I know that full well. My frame was not hidden from you when I was made in the secret place. When I was woven together in the depths of the earth, your eyes saw my unformed body. All the days ordained for me were written in your book before one of them came to

L-R: Alex, Samuel and Julie Armas in late 2003.

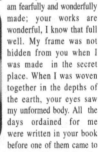

be" (Psalm 139:14-16, NIV). Samuel represents the millions of babies for whom we plead during this year's Sanctity of Human Life Month.

In many ways, 2003 saw positive developments in the pro-life movement on a number of fronts. Referring again to partial-birth abortion, a ban was finally passed by both houses of Congress, despite the outlandish protests of Sen. Boxer, Sen. Kennedy, and Sen. Feinstein. In November, after years and years of frustration and disappointment, President Bush signed the bill into law.[14] Four other pro-family leaders and I met with the President in the Oval Office just prior to the signing, and then witnessed the historic event. Unfortunately, in yet another display of judicial tyranny, three judges immediately issued injunctions to halt the implementation of the law.[15] Nevertheless, we are hopeful that the Supreme Court will declare it to be "Constitutional" in the near future. Please be in prayer about this pivotal decision.

*Each of those children is worth more
than the possessions of the entire world,
and is imbued with an eternal soul that
will live forever in the world to come.*

Now I have some more exciting news to share. It has become increasingly clear to us this year that the Lord is asking us at Focus on the Family and our friends to take a dramatic new step in protecting the preborn child. It will involve the use of a powerful and indispensable tool—ultrasound technology—in the examining rooms of pregnancy resource centers. The available data indicate that 57 percent of women who visit a pregnancy center and report they are considering abortion will decide to keep their baby after going through counseling.[16] However, that number jumps to 79 percent when such women are able to actually see their babies by way of ultrasound images.[17] Unfortunately, only 350 of the 2,300 pregnancy resource centers in our nation currently are able to offer ultrasound services. In light of this reality, Focus on the Family is not content simply to argue for the protection of the unborn. We are now convinced that God is calling us to take an even more dramatic step. Our board of directors has authorized us to help provide ultra-sound equipment to as many centers as possible and help shepherd them through the training and implementation process. How exciting to know that we have it within our sphere of influence to help save thousands of babies every year, each as precious and unique as little Samuel was four years ago! Each of those children is worth more than the possessions of the entire world, and is imbued with an eternal soul that will live forever in the world to come.

Our first-year goal for this new initiative is to help provide 2-D ultrasound machines for 50 pregnancy care centers across the United States. (Newer 4-D ultrasound machines, while offering a clearer image of babies in the womb, are significantly more expensive and therefore may be cost-prohibitive. By embracing 2-D machines—which are still more than adequate in terms of being able to show a living, moving image—we hope to maximize the number of pregnancy care centers that are able to benefit from this technology). Our resources for this project are extremely limited at this point, but we are trusting in the Lord to provide the needed funding because we believe it is such a clear cut and valuable investment. For example, if each of the 50 centers that receives an ultrasound machine this year is able to save even 100 babies as a result, 5,000 lives might be spared! How could we possibly place a price on even one of those children? We hope to expand this initiative dramatically in the coming years as the Lord provides the means to do so. Obviously, your financial help in underwriting our efforts to protect preborn babies would be greatly appreciated. For further information about the benefits of using ultrasound technology in a pregnancy care center environment, or other details about this ambitious initiative, please visit our Web site at family.org/pregnancy.

The good news continues: There are signs that Americans appear to be increasingly embracing a pro-life perspective. A Wirthlin poll released early in 2003 found that 68 percent of respondents favored "restoring legal protection for unborn children," while a similar percentage indicated they would support Supreme Court nominees who favored protections.[18] Similarly, a *USA Today*/CNN/Gallup poll revealed that 70 percent of respondents said that partial-birth abortion should be outlawed, 78 percent backed a mandatory waiting period for all abortions, 73 percent favored parental consent for girls under 18 seeking abortions, and 88 percent favored a law directing doctors to inform patients of alternatives to abortions before they are performed.[19]

Conservative columnist Peggy Noonan made another encouraging observation about the abortion debate last year. In her column for the *Wall Street Journal*, she observed that abortion, which has become the cornerstone issue of liberal ideology, may be the very thing that brings an end to rampant liberalism. "Abortion is now the glue that holds the Democratic Party together," she wrote. "...The abortion rights movement packs huge clout in the party; it can make or break a candidacy with contributions and labor and support... So the pro-abortion forces keep the party together, but they also tie it down. They keep the Democratic Party on the defensive—the lockstep pro-abortion party that won't even back parental notification, the party of unbending orthodoxy that will fight tooth and nail against banning abortions on babies eight months old, babies who look and seem and act exactly like human beings because they are." Ms. Noonan concluded her remarks with this statement that should send chills up the spines of those who continue to see abortion as the highest of virtues: "No party can long endure, or could possibly flourish, with the unfettered killing of young humans as the thing that holds it together."[20] I pray that abortion advocates in *every* political party will carefully reconsider their support of this evil practice.

That day may still be a long way off, however, and there is no denying that there are still a number of challenges and obstacles to overcome in the battle to defend the sanctity of human life. Indeed, the encouraging reports I have shared are tempered by the fact that nearly 45 million babies have been sacrificed since the *Roe v. Wade* decision in 1973. Clearly, we have a long road to travel before human life in <u>all</u> of its expressions—preborn, newborn, elderly, disabled—is embraced and protected.

For those of us who believe that <u>all</u> human life is a gift from God and worthy of protection, though, our mission will remain clear regardless of the shifting tides of public opinion. We will continue to promote legislation that preserves and defends the sanctity of life at every stage, from conception to the grave. With the elections coming up later this year, I hope you will do everything you can to stay informed on this issue. Focus on the Family will be tracking important developments as election season draws near. You can keep updated by logging on to our Web site at www.citizenlink.org. And by all means, see that you are properly registered to vote in November. Not one citizen can afford to sit out this day of decision.

Finally—and even more importantly—I hope you will join me in praying that, regardless of our laws, and regardless of who is in office at any given time, Americans would once again embrace the biblical values upon which our belief in the sanctity of human life is based. As more and more people come to realize that *every* life is important and worthy of protection—whether a developing baby in the womb or an elderly hospice patient who can no longer care for himself or herself—may they gain a newfound awareness of the loving Creator of all life. It's up to us, in our words and deeds, to help make sure that happens. May God grant us strength and resolve for the challenges that lie ahead.

Sincerely,

James C. Dobson

James C. Dobson, Ph.D.
Founder and Chairman

[1] James C. Dobson, Ph.D., "The Picture of the Decade," *Family News*, April 2000. See: http://www.family.org/docstudy/newsletters/a0010560.html
[2] Daniel H. Johnson Jr., M.D. President, American Medical Association, Letter to the Editor, *The New York Times*, 26 May, 1997, p. A22.
[3] "Partial-Birth Abortion Ban Act of 1999," *Congressional Record*, 20 October 1999 (Senate).
See: http://frwebgate4.access.gpo.gov/cgi-bin/waisgate.cgi?WAISdocID=6841455709+0+0+0&WAISaction=retrieve
[4] Ibid.
[5] Ibid.
[6] Ibid.
[7] Ibid.
[8] Ibid.
[9] Ibid.
[10] Ibid.
[11] "Partial-Birth Abortion Ban Act of 2003," *Congressional Record*, 21 October 2003 (Senate).
See: http://frwebgate2.access.gpo.gov/cgi-bin/waisgate.cgi?WAISdocID=685280345413+0+0+0&WAISaction=retrieve
[12] Ibid.
[13] Nat Hentoff, "In the Second Trimester; Who Decides When Human Life Exists?" *The Washington Post*, 24 July 1993, p. A17.
[14] Richard W. Stevenson, "Bush Signs Ban on a Procedure for Abortions," *The New York Times*, 6 November 2003, p. A1.
[15] Anne Gearan, "Abortion Ruling May Not Last," *Deseret News*, 8 November 2003, p. A2.
[16] Focus on the Family Crisis Pregnancy Ministry Ultrasound Research: The Impact of Ultrasound Usage on Abortion-Minded Pregnancy Center Clients, average statistical finding, 26 November 2003. (Internal Follow-Up Telephone Survey.)
[17] Ibid.
[18] Cheryl Wetzstein, "New Poll Shows Tilt To Protect Unborn," *The Washington Times*, 16 January 2003, p. A4.
[19] Kathy Kiely, "Abortion Battle Hits Pivotal Point," *USA Today*, 16 January 2003, p. A6.
[20] Peggy Noonan, "A Tough Roe," *Opinion Journal*, 20 January 2003. See: http://www.opinionjournal.com/columnists/pnoonan/?id=110002936

Publication's title:	Family News From Dr. James Dobson
Issue date:	January 2004
Issue number:	1
Statement of frequency:	Published monthly
Authorized organization's name and address:	Focus on the Family Colorado Springs, CO 80995

This letter may be reproduced without change and in its entirety for non-commercial and non-political purposes without prior permission from Focus on the Family. Copyright © 2004 Focus on the Family. All Rights Reserved. International Copyright Secured. Printed in the U.S.A.

Zeal

Zeal: Passionate ardor in the pursuit of anything. In general, zeal is an eagerness of desire to accomplish or obtain some object, and it may be manifested either in favor of any person or thing, or in opposition to it, and in a good or bad cause.

Enthusiasm: Heat of imagination; violent passion or excitement of the mind in pursuit of some object, inspiring extravagant hope and confidence of success. Hence, the same heat of imagination, chastised by reason or experience, becomes a noble passion, an elevated fancy, a warm imagination, an ardent zeal, that forms sublime ideas, and prompts to the ardent pursuit of laudable (worthy) objects.

Passion: Zeal, ardor, vehement desire. Eager desire, as a violent passion for fine clothes. The feeling of the mind or the sensible effect of impression; excitement, perturbation or agitation of mind; as desire, fear, hope, joy, grief, love, hatred.

> "For ye have heard of my conversation in time past in the Jews' religion, how that beyond measure I persecuted the church of God, and wasted it:" (Galatians 1:13)

> "For I bear them record that they have a zeal of God, but not according to knowledge." (Romans 10:2)

Jesus preached the kingdom of God with zeal, and so did Paul. Yet, I believe the zeal to have been executed with temperance, as stated in Acts 24:25. Jesus preached with zeal, yet also with patience, calmness, and moderation of passion. Prior to Paul's conversion on the road to Damascus, Paul served the Jewish religion with zeal but without knowledge. Paul did not have the knowledge (clear and certain perception) that Christ was the son of God, worthy to be praised, worshipped and adored. Without the proper knowledge, his zeal became misdirected and a threat to true believers, persecuting the church of Christ.

Other scriptures on zeal:

"Whatsoever is commanded by the God of heaven, let it be diligently done for the house of the God of heaven: for why should there be wrath against the realm of the king and his sons?" (Ezra 7:23)

"As many as I love, I rebuke and chasten: be zealous therefore, and repent." (Revelation 3:19)

Mind

❦

Mind: Memory, remembrance, as to put one in mind; to call to mind; the intellectual or intelligent power in man; the understanding; the power that conceives, judges and reasons. I fear I am not in my perfect mind, so we speak of a sound mind… a strong mind with reference to the active powers of understanding; and in a passive sense, it denotes capacity, as when we say, the mind cannot comprehend a subject; the heart or seat of affection.

"For God hath not given us the spirit of fear; but of power, and of love, and of a sound mind." (2 Timothy 1:7)

"For to be carnally minded is death; but to be spiritually minded is life and peace. Because the carnal mind is enmity against God: for it is not subject to the law of God, neither indeed can be." (Romans 8:6-7)

"But if our gospel be hid, it is hid to them that are lost: In whom the god of this world hath blinded the minds of them which believe not, lest the light of the glorious gospel of Christ, who is the image of God, should shine unto them." (2 Corinthians 4:3-4)

God intended that our minds would be strong and be of clear thinking. When Adam and Eve walked in the Garden of Eden with God, this was the case. Their minds were in perfect peace and harmony with God. Their thoughts were clear and unencumbered by fear, sin, shame, confusion, etc. Can you imagine the intellectual power and creativity man would have if he were free of the negative emotions and knowledge of evil that occurred after the original sin? Because man is made in God's image he can do great and wonderful things with his mind. Unfortunately, man must struggle against the evil of his own soul, those who are evil, and the demonic forces of this world.

But original sin was not the end of the story. God sent his son to die on the cross for us to set our minds free of the bondage of sin, to give us hope in the fight against the evil forces of this world. With the power of His word and the help of God, Jesus and the Holy Spirit, God can change our evil minds and shape our minds to be the powerful clear thinking tools they were meant to be. God has also given us an arsenal of weapons to resist and overcome the evil forces that exist in this world. In Ephesians 6, it is mentioned to protect our minds from attack, and even go on the offensive in the battle.

The mind is truly a battleground where good and evil are constantly at war. The devil would like to possess our minds. But the omnipotent power of God through Jesus Christ, and the Holy Spirit have come to set captive minds free. If God be for us, then, who can be against us? Be of good courage! God is with us daily to face each difficulty, each challenge, each evil. If you ask Him, he can strengthen your mind for the battle we face.

It is a sad thing that the unbeliever's mind is spiritually blinded. When Jesus said on the cross "Forgive them for they know not what they do" (Luke 23:34), he was saying, in one sense, their minds are blinded by the gods of this world. They truly couldn't see in their mind's eye that they were killing the Son of God, and the consequence of their action. In Matthew 28:19-20, Jesus said, "go ye therefore and teach all nations, baptizing them in the name of the Holy Ghost teaching them to observe all things whatsoever I have commanded you; and lo I am with you always, even unto the end of the world." Jesus was saying: go, open their minds to the truth that God exists, that I am God's Son, and the commandments I have made for them are for their welfare. We must share the truth of Jesus Christ or their minds/souls are destined for hell.

Other scriptures on the mind:

"And even as they did not like to retain God in their knowledge, God gave them over to a reprobate mind, to do those things which are not convenient;" (Romans 1:28)

Comment: If a homosexual repents, there is still hope for his/her mind/soul.

"Jesus said unto him, Thou shalt love the Lord thy God with all thy heart, and with all thy soul, and with all thy mind." (Matthew 22:37)

"Strip yourselves of your former nature; put off and discard your old unrenewed self, which characterized your previous manner of life and becomes corrupt through lusts and desires that spring from delusion; And be constantly renewed in the spirit of your mind; having a fresh mental and spiritual attitude; And put on the new nature created in God's image, in true righteousness and holiness. (*Amplified Bible Classic Edition*, Ephesians 4:22-24)

Agony

Agony: Extreme pain of body or mind; anguish; appropriately, the pangs of death and the sufferings of our Savior in the garden of Gethsemane.

Pain: an uneasy sensation in animal bodies; of any degree from slight uneasiness to extreme distress or torture, proceeding from pressure, tension or spasm, separation of parts by violence or any derangement of functions. Thus, the violent pressure or stretching of a limb gives pain; inflammation produces pain; wounds, bruises and incisions give pain. Uneasiness of mind; disquietude; anxiety; solicitude (anxiety of the mind) for the future; grief, sorrow for the past. We suffer pain when we fear or expect evil; we feel pain at the loss of friends or property.

Suffer: To feel or bear what is painful, disagreeable or distressing, either to the body or the mind; we suffer pain of body; we suffer grief of mind. The criminal suffers punishment; the sinner suffers pangs of conscience in this life. We suffer wrong; we suffer abuse; we suffer injustice.

> "And being in an agony he prayed more earnestly: and his sweat was as it were great drops of blood falling down to the ground." (Luke 22:44)

> "If we suffer, we shall also reign with him: if we deny him, he also will deny us:" (2 Timothy 2:12)

> "For I will shew him how great things he must suffer for my name's sake." (Acts 9:16)

> "And God shall wipe away all tears from their eyes; and there shall be no more death, neither sorrow, nor crying, neither shall there be any more pain: for the former things are passed away." (Revelation 21:4)

Jesus was in agony just before the crucifixion because of the fear he experienced as a human being, and the evil he expected to face on the cross. He was tempted in all points yet without sin (Hebrews 4:15). Perfect love casts out fear, and Christ faced the fear and evil with courage, casting out the fear. He faced the evil without withdrawing from it. The evil he would face was greater than any man had ever faced. He took all the sins of the world on him. He was marred more than any man and more than the sons of man (Isaiah 52:14). It is no wonder he was in such agony and suffered so in his mind before the cross. Jesus was despised and rejected of men, a man of sorrows acquainted with grief (Isaiah 53:3).

We, as human beings, often suffer in this lifetime. It is the suffering common to man. If we endure suffering, accept him as our Lord and Savior, and do not reject Him, we will reign with Him. I have been in agony of the mind but nothing in comparison to what Christ endured. Jesus suffered unto death, that our sins would be forgiven. What a wonderful Lord and Savior we have. Be grateful for the sacrifice he made for us on the cross. "Greater love hath no man than this, that a man lay down his life for his friends" (John 15:13).

Other scriptures on agony, suffering, or pain:

"For I reckon that the sufferings of this present time are not worthy to be compared with the glory which shall be revealed in us." (Romans 8:18)

"And our hope of you *is* stedfast, knowing, that as ye are partakers of the sufferings, so shall ye be also of the consolation." (2 Corinthians 1:7)

"He is chastened also with pain upon his bed, and the multitude of his bones with strong pain:" (Job 33:19)

Believe

Believe: To have a firm persuasion of anything. In some cases, full persuasion approaching certainty; in others more doubt is implied. It is often followed by in or on, especially in the scriptures. To believe in is to hold as an object of faith. Ye believe in God, believe also in me (John 14:1). To believe on is to trust, to place full confidence in, to rest upon with faith. In theology, to believe sometimes expresses a mere assent of the understanding to the truths of the gospel. In others, the word implies, with this assent of the mind, a yielding of the will and affections, accompanied with a humble reliance on Christ and salvation.

Persuasion: The act of influencing the mind by arguments or reasons offered, or by anything that moves the mind or passions, or inclines the will to a determination. Convinced; settled opinion or conviction proceeding from arguments and reasons offered by others, or suggested by one's own reflections.

> "Then saith he to Thomas, Reach hither thy finger, and behold my hands; and reach hither thy hand, and thrust it into my side: and be not faithless, but believing. And Thomas answered and said unto him, My Lord and my God. Jesus saith unto him, Thomas, because thou hast seen me, thou hast believed: blessed are they that have not seen, and yet have believed. And many other signs truly did Jesus in the presence of his disciples, which are not written in this book: But these are written, that ye might believe that Jesus is the Christ, the Son of God; and that believing ye might have life through his name." (John 20: 27-31)

> "Even so faith, if it hath not works, is dead, being alone. Yea, a man may say, Thou hast faith, and I have works: shew me thy faith without thy works, and I will shew thee

my faith by my works. Thou believest that there is one God; thou doest well: the devils also believe, and tremble. But wilt thou know, O vain man, that faith without works is dead?" (James 2:17-20)

"That if thou shalt confess with thy mouth the Lord Jesus, and shalt believe in thine heart that God hath raised him from the dead, thou shalt be saved. For with the heart man believeth unto righteousness; and with the mouth confession is made unto salvation." (Romans 10:9-10)

There are many reasons I believe in God, Christ, and the Holy Spirit. My mind is persuaded that Jesus is the Son of God, that God exists and is all powerful because of the truth of the Bible, the penetrating truth of Christ's words. I believe in Jesus Christ, the God of Abraham, Isaac, and Jacob and the power and the movement of the Holy Spirit on this earth. The word of God and the words of Jesus Christ have moved my passions and my will, to determine that I am a believer in Jesus Christ. John 20:31 says, "But these are written, that ye might believe that Jesus is the Christ, the Son of God; and that believing ye might have life through his name." God in his grace has given his word to us that we might believe and have everlasting life. James 2:17-20 says, "Even so faith, if it hath not works, is dead, being alone. Yea, a man may say, Thou hast faith, and I have works: shew me thy faith without thy works, and I will shew thee my faith by my works. Thou believest that there is one God; thou doest well: the devils also believe, and tremble. But wilt thou know, O vain man, that faith without works is dead?"

Other scriptures on believing:

"And brought them out, and said, Sirs, what must I do to be saved? And they said, Believe on the Lord Jesus Christ, and thou shalt be saved, and thy house." (Acts 16:30-31)

"So Jonah arose, and went unto Nineveh, according to the word of the Lord. Now Nineveh was an exceeding great city of three days' journey. And Jonah began to enter into the city a day's journey, and he cried, and said, Yet forty days, and Nineveh shall be overthrown. So the people of Nineveh believed God, and proclaimed a fast, and put on sackcloth, from the greatest of them even to the least of them." (Jonah 3:3-5)

"For God so loved the world, that he gave his only begotten Son, that whosoever believeth in him should not perish, but have everlasting life." (John 3:16)

Bondage

Bondage: Slavery or involuntary servitude; captivity; imprisonment; restraint of a person's liberty by compulsion.

Oppressed: Burdened with unreasonable impositions; overpowered, overburdened; depressed.

"He that oppresseth the poor reproacheth his Maker: but he that honoureth him hath mercy on the poor." (Proverbs 14:31)

"Now that which was prepared for me daily was one ox and six choice sheep; also fowls were prepared for me, and once in ten days store of all sorts of wine: yet for all this required not I the bread of the governor, because the bondage was heavy upon this people." (Nehemiah 5:18)

"And they made their lives bitter with hard bondage, in morter, and in brick, and in all manner of service in the field: all their service, wherein they made them serve, was with rigour." (Exodus 1:14)

I will relate a story where my freedom to do that which was right was taken away and how that made me feel. At work, Christians had built shelves to place tracts in so they would be able to share the good news of Jesus Christ. A woman on base complained, and took the base to court. She employed a lawyer from the American Civil Liberties Union (ACLU). She won her case and as a result we had to take down the tract racks. The pastor that taught our Bible study at lunch was asked to leave the base and a room was no longer offered for our Bible study. For over 20 years we had no chaplain on the base. The Christians tried to reason with her and her lawyer. We even offered to allow any faith to put tracts in the racks.

My heart was troubled and I felt oppressed by the event and felt I had to fight back. I tried to think of every alternative to fight this battle, but I was unsaved and naïve, unable to stand against this wrong or to cope with the feelings that arose within me. I had a breakdown – as I had a bad marriage, was flooded out of my house, and Three Mile Island disaster had occurred. But what was meant for evil to take away our freedom to do that which was right, God turned into good. We decided to meet in the cafeteria and take turns teaching the Bible study. As a result we have become more mature in God's word.

One observation I've made in struggling with the issue of freedom is that those who are wicked will fight to oppress that which is right. Conversely the righteous will oppose that which is evil.

Another scriptures on bondage:

"For we wrestle not against flesh and blood, but against principalities, against powers, against the rulers of the darkness of this world, against spiritual wickedness in high places." (Ephesians 6:12)

Comment: There is a spiritual battle going on in this country/ the world.

Busyness

Busy: Employed with constant attention; engaged about something that renders interruption inconvenient; actively employed; occupied without cessation; constantly in motion; as a busy bee.

> "Now it came to pass, as they went, that he entered into a certain village: and a certain woman named Martha received him into her house. And she had a sister called Mary, which also sat at Jesus' feet, and heard his word. But Martha was cumbered about much serving, and came to him, and said, Lord, dost thou not care that my sister hath left me to serve alone? bid her therefore that she help me. And Jesus answered and said unto her, Martha, Martha, thou art careful and troubled about many things: But one thing is needful: and Mary hath chosen that good part, which shall not be taken away from her." (Luke 10:38-42)

Martha had become so busy that her heart became anxious and troubled. If we make our lives too busy, not only do our bodies become tired but also our mind and emotions troubled. This is a fast-moving world and we must employ God's concepts on rest to have an abundant and peaceful life.

I would like to say a word about the busy, demanding lives of pastors. I have a friend in the ministry, where leadership expected him to work long hours. My friend took a stand and said it was affecting his health and taking critical time away from his family. I supported my friend. Another friend's wife had become bitter against Christianity because her father, who was a pastor, in his zeal for the Lord, spent so much time in the ministry that he neglected his daughter. My friend is still trying to lovingly and patiently bring her back to Christ, but the hurt runs deep in her.

Other scriptures on busyness vs. rest:

"Remember the sabbath day, to keep it holy. Six days shalt
thou labour, and do all thy work: But the seventh day is
the sabbath of the Lord thy God: in it thou shalt not do any
work, thou, nor thy son, nor thy daughter, thy manservant,
nor thy maidservant, nor thy cattle, nor thy stranger that is
within thy gates: For in six days the Lord made heaven
and earth, the sea, and all that in them is, and rested the
seventh day: wherefore the Lord blessed the sabbath day,
and hallowed it." (Exodus 20: 8-11)

Comfort

Comfort: To strengthen; to cheer or enliven; To strengthen the mind when depressed or enfeebled; to console; to give new vigor of the spirits; to cheer; or relieve from depression or trouble. (Noun) Relief from pain; ease; rest or moderate pleasure after pain, cold or distress, or uneasiness of the body. The word signifies properly new strength or animation; and relief from pain is often the effect of strength; Relief from distress of the mind; the ease and quiet which is experienced when pain, trouble, agitation or affliction ceases. It implies also some degree of positive animation of the spirits; or some pleasurable sensations derived from hope, and agreeable prospects. That which gives strength or support in distress, difficulty, danger or infirmity.

Consolation: Comfort; alleviation of misery, or distress of mind; refreshment of mind or spirits; a comparative degree of happiness in distress or misfortune, springing from any circumstance that abates the evil, or supports and strengthens the mind, as hope, joy, courage and the like.

"God is our refuge and strength, a very present help in trouble." (Psalm 46:1)

"Cast thy burden upon the Lord, and he shall sustain thee: he shall never suffer the righteous to be moved." (Psalm 55:22)

"Truly my soul waiteth upon God: from him cometh my salvation. He only is my rock and my salvation; he is my defence; I shall not be greatly moved. How long will ye imagine mischief against a man? ye shall be slain all of you: as a bowing wall shall ye be, and as a tottering fence. They only consult to cast him down from his excellency: they delight in lies: they bless with their mouth, but they curse inwardly. Selah. My soul, wait thou only upon God; for my expectation is from him. He only is my rock and my salvation: he is my defence; I shall not be moved. In God is my salvation and my glory: the rock of my strength, and my refuge, is in God. Trust in him at all times; ye people, pour out your heart before him: God is a refuge for us. Selah. Surely men of low degree are vanity, and men of high degree are a lie: to be laid in the balance, they are altogether lighter than vanity. Trust not in oppression, and become not vain in robbery: if riches increase, set not your heart upon them. God hath spoken once; twice have I heard this; that power belongeth unto God. Also unto thee, O Lord, belongeth mercy: for thou renderest to every man according to his work." (Psalm 62:1-12)

There are times when my spirit is low and my troubles are great. During those times, I call upon the Lord, my rock, my refuge, my strength. I depend on my Lord so deeply, for I know that He cares for me and loves me. I pray daily that my God defend and protect my family and my home. My trust is in Him. I call upon Him in times of trouble, for He is my help and my salvation. I believe we must hear the cries of others, and stretch ourselves to help those whose burdens are more than they can bear, to be an encouragement to others. A wise pastor once said to me we are to help carry a person's trunk but not his suitcase. In other words, their daily work is something each person must be responsible for. But, when the trunk is too heavy to carry (their troubles, problems, work, are overburdening), then that is the time to help.

How do we encourage, comfort, and console others? It could be a kind word or a helping hand when someone is overburdened that's needed for renewing their strength. It could be a small child lightening the hearts of the elderly. It could be a pet to lift the spirits. God, His word, and those who follow God's principles must be a comfort and consolation, a light to one another and the world around us.

Other scriptures on comfort/consolation:

"Wherefore comfort yourselves together, and edify one another, even as also ye do." (1 Thessalonians 5:11)

"Remember the word unto thy servant, upon which thou hast caused me to hope. This is my comfort in my affliction: for thy word hath quickened me." (Psalm 119:49-50)

"Yea, though I walk through the valley of the shadow of death, I will fear no evil: for thou art with me; thy rod and thy staff they comfort me." (Psalm 23:4)

Confusion

Confusion: In a general sense, a mixture of several things promiscuously; hence, disorder; irregularity; as the confusion of tongues in Babel.

Confound: To throw into disorder; to perplex or disturb.

Perplexity: Embarrassment of the mind; disturbance from doubt, confusion, difficulty or anxiety.

"For God is not the author of confusion, but of peace, as in all churches of the saints." (1 Corinthians 14:33)

"And it came to pass, that in the morning watch the Lord looked unto the host of the Egyptians through the pillar of fire and of the cloud, and troubled the host of the Egyptians, And took off their chariot wheels, that they drave them heavily: so that the Egyptians said, Let us flee from the face of Israel; for the Lord fighteth for them against the Egyptians." (Exodus 14:24-25)

"There is no peace, saith the Lord, unto the wicked." (Isaiah 48:22)

God can be the author of confusion/trouble to the wicked, as seen with the Egyptians. God can and does trouble and perplex people close to Him. The devil and his minions can also counterfeit what God does. As Christians, we may be knocked down by life but not be without hope or give up. We will feel troubled at times or confused, and at that time we should call upon the Lord to deliver us. As we approach the end times, there will be more and more distress and perplexity in the world. As Christians, we must be a help to those in need, those with troubled hearts. Only by following God's commandments and keeping His word in our hearts can we experience peace in our lives.

Other scriptures on confusion/perplexity:

"We are troubled on every side, yet not distressed; we are perplexed, but not in despair;" (2 Corinthians 4:8)

"These things I have spoken unto you, that in me ye might have peace. In the world ye shall have tribulation: but be of good cheer; I have overcome the world." (John 16:33)

"Peace I leave with you, my peace I give unto you: not as the world giveth, give I unto you. Let not your heart be troubled, neither let it be afraid." (John 14:27)

Conscience

Conscience: Internal or self-knowledge, or judgment of right or wrong; or the faculty, power or principle within us, which decides on the lawfulness or unlawfulness of our own actions and affections, and instantly approves or condemns them. Conscience is called by some writers the moral sense, and considered as an original faculty of our nature. Others question the propriety of considering conscience as a distinct faculty or principle; alleging that our notions of right and wrong are not to be deduced from a single faculty, but from various powers of the understanding and will.

Conviction: The act of convincing, or compelling one to admit the truth of a charge; the state of being convinced or convicted by conscience; the state of being sensible of guilt; as the convictions of a sinner may be temporary, or lasting or efficacious. By conviction a sinner is brought to repentance. Men often sin against the conviction of their own conscience.

Condemn: To pronounce to be utterly wrong; to censure; to blame. But the word often expresses more than censure or blame and includes the idea of utter rejection; as to condemn one's conduct. To determine or judge to be wrong, or guilty; to disallow; to disapprove.

Good: Sound, perfect; uncorrupted; Conformable to moral law; virtuous.

Seared: Burnt on the surface; cauterized; hardened.

Defiled: Made dirty or foul; polluted; soiled; corrupted; violated; vitiated.

> "There is a way that seemeth right unto a man, but the end thereof are the ways of death." (Proverbs 16:25)

> "Now the Spirit speaketh expressly, that in the latter times some shall depart from the faith, giving heed to seducing

spirits, and doctrines of devils; Speaking lies in hypocrisy; having their conscience seared with a hot iron;" (1 Timothy 4:1-2)

"And Paul, earnestly beholding the council, said, Men and brethren, I have lived in all good conscience before God until this day." (Acts 23:1)

Other scriptures on conscience:

"For our rejoicing is this, the testimony of our conscience, that in simplicity and godly sincerity, not with fleshly wisdom, but by the grace of God, we have had our conversation in the world, and more abundantly to you-ward." (2 Corinthians 1:12)

"For when the Gentiles, which have not the law, do by nature the things contained in the law, these, having not the law, are a law unto themselves: Which shew the work of the law written in their hearts, their conscience also bearing witness, and their thoughts the mean while accusing or else excusing one another;" (Romans 2:14-15)

Courage

Courage: Bravery; intrepidity; the quality of mind which enables men to encounter danger and difficulties with firmness, or without fear or depression of spirits; valor; boldness; resolution.

Bravery: Courage; heroism; undaunted spirit; intrepidity; gallantry; fearlessness of danger; often united with generosity or dignity of mind which despises meanness and cruelty, and disdains to take advantage of a vanquished enemy.

Boldness: Courage; bravery; intrepidity; spirit; fearlessness.

"Be strong and of a good courage, fear not, nor be afraid of them: for the Lord thy God, he it is that doth go with thee; he will not fail thee, nor forsake thee." (Deuteronomy 31:6)

"Be strong and of a good courage: for unto this people shalt thou divide for an inheritance the land, which I sware unto their fathers to give them." (Joshua 1:6)

"The wicked flee when no man pursueth: but the righteous are bold as a lion." (Proverbs 28:1)

When David faced Goliath, he did it courageously. When Sampson faced one thousand Philistines with only the jawbone of an ass, he did it with courage. When Stephen was about to be stoned, he faced his impending death with courage. When Jesus faced death on the cross, he faced it courageously. Daniel in the Lion's den faced great danger. Shadrach, Meshach, and Abednego were thrown into a fiery furnace. How did these men face danger, pain, evil, suffering, and death with such courage? They did so, knowing that God was with them and that He would never fail them or forsake them. At one point in my life, I felt that evil was all around me. A Christian counselor said "God would be insulted if you thought evil was greater than Him." I realized God is all-powerful and able to protect us through any danger if He chooses. The words of the Bible, and the above examples, give us all a view of true courage and how we can face such situations.

Other scriptures on courage:

"The Lord is my light and my salvation; whom shall I fear? the Lord is the strength of my life; of whom shall I be afraid?" (Psalm 27:1)

"Have not I commanded thee? Be strong and of a good courage; be not afraid, neither be thou dismayed: for the Lord thy God is with thee whithersoever thou goest." (Joshua 1:9)

"If it be so, our God whom we serve is able to deliver us from the burning fiery furnace, and he will deliver us out of thine hand, O king. But if not, be it known unto thee, O king, that we will not serve thy gods, nor worship the golden image which thou hast set up." (Daniel 3:17-18)

Decide

Decide: To determine; to form a definite opinion; to come to a conclusion. Determination of a course of action.

Determine: To resolve; to conclude; to come to a decision.

Determination: Decision of a question in the mind; firm resolution; settled purpose.

"For to do whatsoever thy hand and thy counsel determined before to be done." (Acts 4:28)

"Then the disciples, every man according to his ability, determined to send relief unto the brethren which dwelt in Judaea:" (Acts 11:29)

I have decided or determined, for now, to follow the doctor's counsel regarding the dosage of medication. This decision does not come easy. The medication, which is supposed to help, has also caused me harm. The spasms at night, the tightness of the muscles (sometimes unbearable), the hard heartedness I experienced with the over-dosage, the apathy, the loss of feelings – I consider all to be harmful effects. Where to draw the line is not an easy decision. I have to decide whether I need the medication at all. God knows, but I don't believe anyone else knows. Without feelings to guide me, I must decide, based on what I know. Life for me has not been easy on medication. For whatever reason, God has allowed me to experience this. I decide by weighing the alternatives, but mostly through prayer, hoping God will guide me in each decision I make. After going off my medication with the doctor's supervision, I had another breakdown. I knew for sure that I must have the medication. With God's help, the decision was made and the dosage made bearable.

Other scriptures on decisions or determination:

"For Paul had determined to sail by Ephesus, because he would not spend the time in Asia: for he hasted, if it were possible for him, to be at Jerusalem the day of Pentecost." (Acts 20:16)

"And Solomon determined to build an house for the name of the Lord, and an house for his kingdom." (2 Chronicles 2:1)

Doubt

Doubt: To waiver or fluctuate in opinion; to hesitate; to be in suspense; to be in uncertainty, respecting the truth or fact; to be undetermined. Even in matters of divine, concerning some things, we may lawfully doubt and suspend judgment. A fluctuation of mind respecting truth or propriety, arising from a defect of knowledge or evidence; uncertainty of mind; suspense; unsettled state of opinion; as to have doubts respecting the theory of the tides. Suspicion; fear; apprehension. I stand in doubt of you (Galatians 4). Uncertainty of condition. Thy life shall hang in doubt before thee.

> "And Gideon said unto God, If thou wilt save Israel by mine hand, as thou hast said, Behold, I will put a fleece of wool in the floor; and if the dew be on the fleece only, and it be dry upon all the earth beside, then shall I know that thou wilt save Israel by mine hand, as thou hast said. And it was so: for he rose up early on the morrow, and thrust the fleece together, and wringed the dew out of the fleece, a bowl full of water. And Gideon said unto God, Let not thine anger be hot against me, and I will speak but this once: let me prove, I pray thee, but this once with the fleece; let it now be dry only upon the fleece, and upon all the ground let there be dew. And God did so that night: for it was dry upon the fleece only, and there was dew on all the ground." (Judges 6:36-40)
>
> "And Gideon said unto him, Oh my Lord, if the Lord be with us, why then is all this befallen us? and where be all his miracles which our fathers told us of, saying, Did not the Lord bring us up from Egypt? but now the Lord hath forsaken us, and delivered us into the hands of the Midianites. And the Lord looked upon him, and said, Go in this thy might, and thou shalt save Israel from the hand of the Midianites: have not I sent thee? And he said unto

him, Oh my Lord, wherewith shall I save Israel? behold, my family is poor in Manasseh, and I am the least in my father's house." (Judges 6:13-15)

"And Moses said unto God, Who am I, that I should go unto Pharaoh, and that I should bring forth the children of Israel out of Egypt?" (Exodus 3:11)

Both Moses and Gideon doubted that they were the ones who should answer God's calling to save the Israeli people. Many times our doubt, or unbelief, comes from within ourselves. But Satan can also cause our unbelief. Recently, my son got a new job. I prayed all would go well with him in this new job. After I prayed, I found out that he had some doubts and lacked some confidence in his ability to do the job. He shared with me that during the time that I prayed he gained more confidence in himself. Today he's third in command at a large prosperous restaurant.

Other scriptures on doubt or unbelief:

"And the serpent said unto the woman, Ye shall not surely die:" (Genesis 3:4)

"Now while Peter doubted in himself what this vision which he had seen should mean, behold, the men which were sent from Cornelius had made enquiry for Simon's house, and stood before the gate, And called, and asked whether Simon, which was surnamed Peter, were lodged there. While Peter thought on the vision, the Spirit said unto him, Behold, three men seek thee. Arise therefore, and get thee down, and go with them, doubting nothing: for I have sent them." (Acts 10:17-20)

"And he said, Come. And when Peter was come down out of the ship, he walked on the water, to go to Jesus. But when he saw the wind boisterous, he was afraid; and beginning to sink, he cried, saying, Lord, save me. And immediately Jesus stretched forth his hand, and caught him, and said unto him, O thou of little faith, wherefore didst thou doubt?" (Matthew 14:29-31)

"I desire to be present with you now, and to change my voice; for I stand in doubt of you." (Galatians 4:20)

Encourage

Encourage: Inspire with hope and confidence; exciting courage. To furnish grounds to hope for success. To inspire with courage, spirit, or strength of mind; to embolden; to animate; to incite.

Encouragement: The act of giving courage, or confidence of success; incitement to action or to practice; incentive. The praise of good men serves as an encouragement of virtue and heroism.

> "But charge Joshua, and encourage him, and strengthen him: for he shall go over before this people, and he shall cause them to inherit the land which thou shalt see." (Deuteronomy 3:28)

> "And David was greatly distressed; for the people spake of stoning him, because the soul of all the people was grieved, every man for his sons and for his daughters: but David encouraged himself in the Lord his God." (1 Samuel 30:6)

> "And he set the priests in their charges, and encouraged them to the service of the house of the Lord," (2 Chronicles 35:2)

I believe we are not only called to be courageous, but to encourage (give courage, hope or confidence) others. Exodus 14:13 says, "And Moses said unto the people, fear ye not, stand still and see the salvation of the Lord which he will show you today, for the Egyptians whom ye have seen today ye shall see them again no more." Encouragement can come in many forms. It can come from kind words, such as picking out one good thing a person does and praising him for it. It can come from supplying financial help in time of need, or providing badly needed resources. Encouragement can come by providing good news when someone is feeling down. The Bible is often called the good news of Jesus Christ. It can come from providing possibilities of a breakthrough for a difficult problem. It can come in the form of support, by accompanying a person to a meeting to obtain a goal. It can come from an act of love or generosity. It can come from bringing someone joy, or by giving a gift. It can come by providing someone temporary residence until they can get back on their feet. Life is tough and it's getting tougher. If 9/11 is an indication of what's to come, we must encourage one another to get through it.

For those with mental illness, it seems that there is no hope. But I can personally testify that there is. Matthew 19:26 says, "But Jesus beheld them and said unto them, with men this is impossible, but with God all things are possible." Mark 9:17-23 says,

> "And one of the multitude answered and said, Master, I have brought unto thee my son, And wheresoever he taketh him, he teareth him: and he foameth, and gnasheth his teeth, and pineth (to lose flesh or to wear away under any distress or anxiety of the mind) away; and I spake to thy disciples that they should cast him out and they could not. He answereth him and saith, O faithless generation, how long shall I be with you? Bring him unto me. And they brought him unto him, straightway the spirit tare him; and he fell on the ground and wallowed foaming. And he asked his father, How long is it ago since this came unto him? And he said, Of a child. And oftimes it hath cast him into the waters, to destroy him: but if thou canst do anything, have compassion on us. And Jesus said unto him, if thou canst believe, all things are possible to him that believeth."

This is a message of hope for parents with children who are mentally ill. Ask God for help for your son or daughter as this parent did. Always pray and never give up.

Other scriptures on encouragement:

"So the carpenter encouraged the goldsmith, and he that smootheth with the hammer him that smote the anvil, saying, It is ready for the sodering: and he fastened it with nails, that it should not be moved." (Isaiah 41:7)

Examination of the Heart

Examination: Mental inquiry; careful consideration of the circumstances or facts which relate to a subject or question; a view of the qualities and relations, and an estimate of their nature and importance.

Consider: To fix the mind on, with a view of careful examination; to think on with care; to ponder; to study; to meditate on.

Humility: In ethics, freedom from pride and arrogance; humbleness of mind; a modest estimate of one's worth. In theology, humility consists in lowliness of mind; a deep sense of one's unworthiness in the sight of God, self-abasement, penitence for sin, and submission to the divine will.

"But by the grace of God I am what I am: and his grace which was bestowed upon me was not in vain; but I laboured more abundantly than they all: yet not I, but the grace of God which was with me." (1 Corinthians 15:10)

"Not that we are sufficient of ourselves to think any thing as of ourselves; but our sufficiency is of God;"(2 Corinthians 3:5)

"Then Jesus went with them. And when he was now not far from the house, the centurion sent friends to him, saying unto him, Lord, trouble not thyself: for I am not worthy that thou shouldest enter under my roof:" (Luke 7:6)

"But God forbid that I should glory, save in the cross of our Lord Jesus Christ, by whom the world is crucified unto me, and I unto the world." (Galatians 6:14)

As I ponder who I am in Christ, I realize how unworthy I am in thought, motivation, and deed. God, in a mysterious way, showed me how so many of my thoughts are wrong and unrighteous. Yet, I try my best to bring every thought captive unto Christ. God has humbled me. I am not worthy of salvation, save by the death of Christ on the cross.

When I have sufficient time to consider my motivations and determine what is right or wrong, I do a better job of having pure motivations. It does not always come naturally. When I have had insufficient time to examine my motivations, I have sometimes failed miserably. I am a sinner. Unless for Christ's sacrifice on the cross, my soul would be lost.

In deed, even after careful consideration, I sometimes choose wrong. If salvation were determined by a perfect adherence to the law, we would all be lost. God's word guides us in our attempt to fulfill the principles of God, His love, grace, and mercy, and finish what we cannot do on our own, by bringing us unto salvation. When I examine myself, I realize my lowliness and God's exaltation. His thoughts are higher than our thoughts, His ways higher than our ways.

I once had a counselor say, "I never met anyone that is OK." In a sense, he's right. We are all sinners. Yet, if we take the idea one step further, we are OK because of Christ's sacrifice for us on the cross. So, when someone passes me in the hall and asks me how I am, I can truthfully, in my heart, say I'm OK.

Comment: Communion is the perfect time to examine our hearts before God.

Other scriptures on humility:

"What is man, that thou art mindful of him? and the son of man, that thou visitest him?" (Psalm 8:4)

"By humility and the fear of the Lord are riches, and honour, and life."(Proverbs 22:4)

"But he giveth more grace. Wherefore he saith, God resisteth the proud, but giveth grace unto the humble." (James 4:6)

"Humble yourselves in the sight of the Lord, and he shall lift you up." (James 4:10)

Forget

Forget: To lose remembrance; to let go from memory.

Forgetful: Apt to forget; easily losing the remembrance of. A forgetful man should use helps to strengthen his memory.

Remembrance: The retaining or having in mind an idea which had been present before. Technically, remembrance differs from reminiscence and recollection, as the former implies an idea occurs to the mind spontaneously, or without much mental exertion. The latter imply the power or act of recalling ideas which do not spontaneously recur to the mind.

> "Beware that thou forget not the Lord thy God, in not keeping his commandments, and his judgments, and his statutes, which I command thee this day:" (Deuteronomy 8:11)

> "My son, forget not my law; but let thine heart keep my commandments:" (Proverbs 3:1)

> "And I looked, and rose up, and said unto the nobles, and to the rulers, and to the rest of the people, Be not ye afraid of them: remember the Lord, which is great and terrible, and fight for your brethren, your sons, and your daughters, your wives, and your houses." (Nehemiah 4:14)

I prayed and asked the Lord what subject I should write about next. I had been somewhat forgetful lately and God impressed on me this was what he wanted me to write about. I received confirmation of this when a second prayer of mine was answered. I had prayed and asked the Lord what plants I should plant with my testimonial stone. I recently received two packets of "forget-me-not" seeds to plant, one from my father and one from someone handing out packets asking for support for a local election. Forget-me-not is what God is asking us to do—don't forget God! As an affluent country, we sometimes forget the source of our wealth and prosperity—the Lord. God's word tells us to ask Him and He will protect and fight for our brothers, our sons and our daughters, our wives and our houses. In these times of worldwide terrorism, it is so important that we remember our God, His word and to live out His principles in our lives. There are deadly consequences in forgetting our God, too terrible to contemplate. "Forget-me-not" says our Lord and savior Jesus Christ. Forget me not!!!

Other scriptures on forget:

"Be not forgetful to entertain strangers: for thereby some have entertained angels unawares." (Hebrews 13:2)

"Bless the Lord, O my soul, and forget not all his benefits:" (Psalm 103:2)

"I will never forget thy precepts: for with them thou hast quickened me." (Psalm 119:93)

"Brethren, I count not myself to have apprehended: but this one thing I do, forgetting those things which are behind, and reaching forth unto those things which are before, I press toward the mark for the prize of the high calling of God in Christ Jesus." (Philippians 3:13-14)

Freedom

Freedom: A state of exemption from the power or control of another; liberty; exemption from slavery, servitude or confinement.

Liberty: Freedom from restraint, in a general sense, and applicable to the body, or to the will or mind. The body is at liberty when not confined; the will or mind is at liberty when not checked or controlled. A man enjoys liberty, when no physical force operates to restrain his actions or volitions.

> "And ye shall know the truth, and the truth shall make you free." (John 8:32)

> "If the Son therefore shall make you free, ye shall be free indeed." (John 8:36)

> "The Spirit of the Lord God is upon me; because the Lord hath anointed me to preach good tidings unto the meek; he hath sent me to bind up the brokenhearted, to proclaim liberty to the captives, and the opening of the prison to them that are bound;" (Isaiah 61:1)

I spoke to my prison ministry about freedom. There can be physical freedom, freedom of our emotions, and freedom of our mind and spirit. I asked them not to dwell on the physical bondage they were in, but to think on the freedom of the mind, emotions, and spirit they had. When they accepted Christ as their savior, their spirits became free. When they turned away from sin and repented, their minds and emotions became free. We, as Christians, can be oppressed in our hearts and souls but not possessed – as the unbeliever can. I asked them to dwell on the scripture that says, "Whatsoever things are just, whatsoever things are honest, whatsoever things are pure, whatsoever things are lovely, whatsoever things are of good report; if there be any virtue, if there be any praise, think on these things" (Philippians 4:8).

Other scriptures on freedom or liberty:

"Now the Lord is that Spirit: and where the Spirit of the Lord is, there is liberty." (2 Corinthians 3:17)

"I will run the way of thy commandments, when thou shalt enlarge my heart." (Psalm 119:32)

Harshness

Harsh: Rough to the touch; Rough, rude; abusive as harsh words.

Rough: Rugged of temper; severe; austere; rude; not mild or courteous. Generally, harsh or rough words or actions can generate feelings of anxiety, anger, or rejection by the one hearing those words or receiving those actions, causing him or her to feel unloved.

"He that spareth his rod hateth his son: but he that loveth him chasteneth him betimes." (Proverbs 13:24)

"Submitting yourselves one to another in the fear of God." (Ephesians 5:21)

"Children, obey your parents in the Lord: for this is right. Honour thy father and mother; which is the first commandment with promise; That it may be well with thee, and thou mayest live long on the earth. And, ye fathers, provoke not your children to wrath: but bring them up in the nurture and admonition of the Lord." (Ephesians 6:1-4)

My wife has said I have been harsh at times. Although harshness is not a good thing and should be avoided, there are many pressures in our lives that could cause us to be harsh when under normal circumstances we wouldn't be. One of my favorite movies is "It's a Wonderful Life" with Jimmy Stewart. For most of his character's life in the movie, he served others, denied himself, and cared about the welfare of others. He stood up for the weak against a cruel and greedy, rich man who owned most of the town assets. His uncle worked with him in the savings and loan department.

One day, his uncle misplaced a large sum of money while taking it to the bank. They looked everywhere for the money, but that rich man had found it and not returned it. Jimmy's character, George Bailey, said he wouldn't take the fall for his uncle, but in his heart he knew he would spare him, as his uncle was weaker and probably couldn't handle it. He went to the cruel rich man and asked if he would provide the money, using his insurance policy as collateral, but the rich man accused him of embezzling the money and called the police. George was about to break, as the whole world around him seemed harsh. In one short moment, he uttered some harsh words to his children. Although George's words were wrong, I felt compassion for him. That was not how he wanted to act and he immediately apologized. His wife defended the children, but knew in her heart there was something deeper bothering her husband. After George left, she began to inquire of others what had happened. She immediately supported her husband by seeking the help of the townspeople, and she was able to get through to George's rich friend. I love what his wife did for him. I can't think of a more loving way to respond to a husband in need or in trouble.

My wife and I have disagreed on the level of discipline we should show our child. I believe men were created with a rougher, tougher, harsher nature. The man has the protective role for the family. A woman, on the other hand, was built more tenderhearted, as the comforter, as the nurturer of the family. By themselves, the roles of disciplinarians are incomplete. Each should complement one another and a compromise should be reached. If discipline is too harsh, a grudge may develop in the child. If all three of the above scriptures are applied, I believe the end result is a disciplinary action that is not too harsh but will rather guide him or her to be a responsible citizen of society. As a parent, it is difficult to discipline my child but I have to do what's right for the child and prevent the development of a rebellious, disrespectful being; a child that may develop a destructive spirit if not taught right from wrong.

Other scriptures on roughness, harshness:

"And Joseph saw his brethren, and he knew them, but made himself strange unto them, and spake roughly unto them; and he said unto them, Whence come ye? And they said, From the land of Canaan to buy food." (Genesis 42:7)

"Then said David to Jonathan, Who shall tell me? or what if thy father answer thee roughly?" (1 Samuel 20:10)

"And the king answered the people roughly, and forsook the old men's counsel that they gave him;" (1 Kings 12:13)

Inspiration

Inspiration: The infusion of ideas into the mind by the Holy Spirit, the conveying into the minds of men ideas, notices or monitions by extraordinary or supernatural influence; or communication of the divine will to the understanding by suggestions or impressions on the mind, which leave no doubt the reality of the supernatural origin.

> "And after the earthquake a fire; but the Lord was not in the fire: and after the fire a still small voice. And it was so, when Elijah heard it, that he wrapped his face in his mantle, and went out, and stood in the entering in of the cave. And, behold, there came a voice unto him, and said, What doest thou here, Elijah?" (1 Kings 19:12-13)

> "Now therefore go, and I will be with thy mouth, and teach thee what thou shalt say." (Exodus 4:12)

> "All scripture is given by inspiration of God, and is profitable for doctrine, for reproof, for correction, for instruction in righteousness: That the man of God may be perfect, thoroughly furnished unto all good works." (2 Timothy 3:16-17)

God's word has inspired me to write this book, and through various methods, infused ideas into my mind as to what to write. I was having many doubts as to why it seemed God had forsaken me with regard to the topic of wisdom. It was an uneasy, unsettled time. It was during this time God spoke to me in a still, small voice. He only spoke one word: doubt. God inspired me to write about doubt through this still small voice.

There have been times I have had to speak publicly. During these times, I asked the Lord to give me a peace as I spoke and to guide my words and let my words be God's words. 2 Timothy 3:16 says, "all scripture is given by inspiration of

God." There is no doubt in me the truth of these words. God's word has inspired people to love others, to sacrifice for others, to lay down their lives for others. "Greater love hath no man than this, that a man lay down his life for his friends" (John 15:13). And yet Jesus laid down his life for us while we were yet sinners. God's word truly does inspire others to do great things and will continue to inspire people throughout eternity.

Other scriptures on inspiration:

"For the prophecy came not in old time by the will of man: but holy men of God spake as they were moved by the Holy Ghost." (2 Peter 1:21)

"And the Spirit of the Lord began to move him at times in the camp of Dan between Zorah and Eshtaol." (Judges 13:25)

Know

Know: To perceive with certainty; to understand clearly; to have a clear and certain perception of truth, fact or anything that actually exists.

Knowledge: A clear and certain perception of that which exists, or of truth and fact. God has a perfect knowledge of all his works. Human knowledge is very limited, and is mostly gained by observation and experience.

"And ye shall know the truth, and the truth shall make you free." (John 8:32)

"Be still, and know that I am God: I will be exalted among the heathen, I will be exalted in the earth." (Psalm 46:10)

"The heart of him that hath understanding seeketh knowledge: but the mouth of fools feedeth on foolishness." (Proverbs 15:14)

There are many things I do not know, but one thing that I do know is that there is a God. I know there is a God because he has spoken to me in a still small voice. I know there is a God because of the many answered prayers. I know there is a God, because His word testifies to my heart. I know there is a God, because of the intelligent design in His creation; the trees, the earth, the human body, the universe. I know Him intimately through His word. This knowing has created a strong relationship with Him. This knowledge and relationship make me free from the penalty of sin, and spiritual death. What I do not know, I seek to know. I study and I pray for wisdom and understanding, and seek out knowledge.

Other scriptures on knowing, knowledge:

"But thou, O Daniel, shut up the words, and seal the book, even to the time of the end: many shall run to and fro, and knowledge shall be increased." (Daniel 12:4)

"Give a portion to seven, and also to eight; for thou knowest not what evil shall be upon the earth." (Ecclesiastes 11:2)

"When I cry unto thee, then shall mine enemies turn back: this I know; for God is for me." (Psalm 56:9)

"I applied mine heart to know, and to search, and to seek out wisdom, and the reason of things, and to know the wickedness of folly, even of foolishness and madness:" (Ecclesiastes 7:25)

"For I know that my redeemer liveth, and that he shall stand at the latter day upon the earth: And though after my skin worms destroy this body, yet in my flesh shall I see God:" (Job 19:25-26)

Malice

Malice: Extreme enmity of heart or malevolence; a disposition to injure others without cause, from mere personal gratification, or from a spirit of revenge.

Malevolence: Having an evil disposition towards another; ill will; personal hatred; enmity of heart; inclination to injure others.

Enmity: The quality of being an enemy; the opposite of friendship; ill will; hatred; a state of opposition.

"Let all bitterness, and wrath, and anger, and clamour, and evil speaking, be put away from you, with all malice:" (Ephesians 4:31)

"Rejoiceth not in iniquity, but rejoiceth in the truth;" (1 Corinthians 13:6)

I have a Christian friend that had been treated badly, and as we talked, it was clear she wanted justice done and thought she might find joy in that. But something troubled her. I related a story to her that my Christian counselor had told me when I questioned him on a similar situation. He said "imagine that during World War II, two Japanese soldiers are holding an American prisoner. The boat capsizes and the two Japanese soldiers drown. The American escapes and swims to safety." He said, "the way we should feel is joy, that the American escaped, but sadness over the death of the Japanese soldiers. Life is precious and they probably didn't know Christ. If one were to find joy in the death of the Japanese soldiers, this would be a feeling of malice or malevolence." Colossians 3:8 says, "But now ye also put off all these: anger, wrath, malice, blasphemy, and filthy communications out of your mouth."

Other scriptures on malice:

"For we ourselves also were sometimes foolish, disobedient, deceived, serving divers lusts and pleasures, living in malice and envy, hateful, and hating one another." (Titus 3:3)

"Wherefore laying aside all malice, and all guile, and hypocrisies, and envies, and all evil speakings, As new-born babes, desire the sincere milk of the word, that ye may grow thereby:" (1 Peter 2:1-2)

Perceive

Perceive: To have knowledge or receive impressions of external objects through the medium of the senses or bodily organs.

Sense: Perception by the intellect; apprehension; discernment; The faculty of the soul by which it perceives external objects by means of impressions made on certain organs of the body.

Sensitive: Having sense or feeling, or having the capacity of perceiving impressions from external objects.

"Yet the Lord hath not given you an heart to perceive, and eyes to see, and ears to hear, unto this day." (Deuteronomy 29:4)

"For I perceive that thou art in the gall of bitterness, and in the bond of iniquity." (Acts 8:23)

"Then Peter opened his mouth, and said, Of a truth I perceive that God is no respecter of persons: But in every nation he that feareth him, and worketh righteousness, is accepted with him." (Acts 10:34-35)

I have experienced distorted perception on the following occasions and I believe the first occurred at my breakdown. My home had just been flooded by the Yellow Breeches Creek, and I lost my job. The emotional stress of a failing marriage and the confusion of who to trust during the Three Mile Island disaster, were too much for me. I believe all of these stressors led to my breakdown. I experienced paranoia. I believe there was healing, but a number of years later I had another distortion of my perception. I felt overwhelmed at work. I began to feel my boss was coming against me, but my vision had a severe distortion. I had a talk with my boss, whose kind words brought me out of it.

I believe people's perceptions to be very strong, but it is a sense – just like any other sense – and only gives us part of the picture, as our emotions do. When our emotions and our mind are overloaded and can't handle any more, there is damage to them. Each time I experienced a breakdown in my perception, I was under a great deal of stress.

I had a conversation with my boss and we discussed the fact that I was very sensitive. I told him it can be a blessing or a curse. It can be a blessing, in that I can sense the love someone has for me. It can be a curse, in that I can sense when someone doesn't like me and that hurts. I am also sensitive to good and evil and that can be a blessing and a curse.

Other scriptures on perception, sensitivity:

"And Samuel arose, and gat him up from Gilgal unto Gibeah of Benjamin. And Saul numbered the people that were present with him, about six hundred men. And Saul, and Jonathan his son, and the people that were present with them, abode in Gibeah of Benjamin: but the Philistines encamped in Michmash. And the spoilers came out of the camp of the Philistines in three companies: one company turned unto the way that leadeth to Ophrah, unto the land of Shual:" (1 Samuel 13:15-17)

Reason

Reasoning: The act or process of exercising the faculty of reason; that act or operation of the mind by which new or unknown propositions are deduced from previous ones which are known and evident, or which are admitted or supposed for the sake of argument; as fair reasoning; false reasoning; absurd reasoning; strong or weak reasoning. The reasoning of the advocate appeared to the court conclusive.

Reason: That which is thought or alleged in words as the ground or cause of opinion, conclusion or determination. I have reasons which I may choose not to disclose. I freely give my reasons. The cause, ground, principle or motive of anything said or done; that which supports or justifies a determination, plan or measure.

"Come now, and let us reason together, saith the Lord: though your sins be as scarlet, they shall be as white as snow; though they be red like crimson, they shall be as wool." (Isaiah 1:18)

"Now therefore stand still, that I may reason with you before the Lord of all the righteous acts of the Lord, which he did to you and to your fathers." (1 Samuel 12:7)

I would like to relate a story where my wife and I went through the reasoning process and I initially felt rejected by my wife. Her reasons for wanting to act were good, so why did I feel rejection? I have been renovating our basement, putting in a new bathroom, and purchasing a microwave and a small refrigerator. The reason I am doing so is because I feel hard times are coming to the United States.

David Wilkerson and other Christian leaders have foreseen for some time the financial collapse and hardship coming to the United States. Larry Burkett wrote a book called the Economic Earthquake, where he foresaw the financial downfall of the United States. Other Christian modern-day prophets, or prophecy experts, such as Hal Lindsay and Grant Jeffrey have indicated similar beliefs. Pat Robertson said on his show that he believes as he went to pray to God, there would be rampant violence in the U.S. and then God's judgment would fall on the United States. Only time will tell if these prophesies will come true, however, it's not hard to understand how these events might transpire, as we look at what happened on 9/11.

We've seen some of the violence already. Fanatical Muslims hate Christians and Jews and the United States. Osama Bin Laden struck one of our strong financial centers, I believe to destroy our country economically. I have been improving my basement to possibly help a family in the coming hard times. If nothing happens, I've just gained improvements in my home.

The rejection I felt was when my wife said she was talking to a friend and briefly mentioned we had a washer available. A camp was in need of one, so she said she'd discuss it with me. Her desire to do good flew in opposition to what I felt God was leading me to do. I felt rejected because she had refused to receive my charitable idea. Truthfully, I had other reasons for wanting to keep the washer. In submarines, they often have two or more back-up systems in the event one fails. We have had a number of appliance failures, so I thought it was a good idea to keep an extra. Regardless, I conceded to her wishes.

Other scriptures on reason:

"Surely I would speak to the Almighty, and I desire to reason with God." (Job 13:3)

"But when Jesus perceived their thoughts, he answering said unto them, What reason ye in your hearts?" (Luke 5:22)

"And Paul, as his manner was, went in unto them, and three sabbath days reasoned with them out of the scriptures," (Acts 17:2)

Rejection

Rejection: The act of throwing away; the act of casting off or forsaking; refusal to accept or grant.

Reject: To throw away as anything useless or vile; to cast off; to refuse to receive; to slight; to despise; to refuse to accept.

"And he began to teach them, that the Son of man must suffer many things, and be rejected of the elders, and of the chief priests, and scribes, and be killed, and after three days rise again." (Mark 8:31)

"But the Pharisees and lawyers rejected the counsel of God against themselves, being not baptized of him." (Luke 7:30)

At work, there have been a number of people I have tried to reach out to, in love, but that love and acceptance was not returned. I believe I was feeling rejection. Was it these people's lack of capacity to receive the love and return it, or was it my inability to give my love for them and to love them properly? Being less than perfect human beings, it was probably some degree of both. Christ was rejected more than any other man. When Pontius Pilate asked who do you want to release from the pain, suffering, and death on the cross: Barabbas or Jesus. They chose Barabbas. The people rejected Jesus unto death. It's hard to conceive of a greater rejection than that. It was hard for Jesus and it's hard for anyone that feels rejected.

How did Jesus handle the rejection? He continued to love them unto death. He said "Forgive them for they know not what they do." Christ had forgiven them in His heart and through His great love for mankind, took that forgiveness one step further and interceded for them with God. How hard that must have been for Him in His humanness, but Christ was more than human and was able to show a love so great, it is difficult to fully understand or comprehend. Sometimes we in our own strength are not able to forgive and we should and must call upon God to help us to forgive totally.

I feel no rejection from Jesus Christ. He has left me with a feeling of love and acceptance. He has left me with a feeling of great love for Him, that there is no denying the existence of God for me.

Other scriptures on rejection:

"Saying, The Son of man must suffer many things, and be rejected of the elders and chief priests and scribes, and be slain, and be raised the third day." (Luke 9:22)

"Jesus cried and said, He that believeth on me, believeth not on me, but on him that sent me. And he that seeth me seeth him that sent me. I am come a light into the world, that whosoever believeth on me should not abide in darkness. And if any man hear my words, and believe not, I judge him not: for I came not to judge the world, but to save the world. He that rejecteth me, and receiveth not my words, hath one that judgeth him: the word that I have spoken, the same shall judge him in the last day. For I have not spoken of myself; but the Father which sent me, he gave me a commandment, what I should say, and what I should speak. And I know that his commandment is life everlasting: whatsoever I speak therefore, even as the Father said unto me, so I speak." (John 12:44-50)

Remember

Remembrance: The retaining or having in mind an idea which had been present before. Technically, remembrance differs from reminiscence and recollection, as the former implies an idea occurs to the mind spontaneously or without much mental exertion. The latter imply the power or act of recalling ideas which do not spontaneously recur to the mind.

Remember: To have in mind an idea which had been in mind before.

> "And I looked, and rose up, and said unto the nobles, and to the rulers, and to the rest of the people, Be not ye afraid of them: remember the Lord, which is great and terrible, and fight for your brethren, your sons, and your daughters, your wives, and your houses." (Nehemiah 4:14)

I remember many good things in my life. I remember my friends, my canoe trips down the Little Conestoga, to the Big Conestoga, and to the Susquehanna River. It was a fifteen-mile trip. We were young teenagers, and what an adventure it was. We braved rapids, portaged when necessary, and swam in the creeks for refreshment. It took about a whole day, and my father and neighbors would pick us up at the end of our trip. What fun we had splashing each other and with camaraderie. It's something I'll remember fondly for years to come.

Other scriptures on remember:

> "Remember the sabbath day, to keep it holy." (Exodus 20:8)

> "Some trust in chariots, and some in horses: but we will remember the name of the Lord our God." (Psalm 20:7)

Respect

Respect: Consideration, courteous regard; as one must have respect for the feelings of others. To feel or show honor to; to consider or treat with deference or courtesy.

Thoughtful: Attentive; especially considerate of others.

Attentive: Implies a constant thoughtfulness as shown with repeated acts of consideration.

Considerate: Having or showing regard for others and their feelings or circumstances as in sparing them pain, distress or discomfort.

Revere: To regard with reverence; to regard with fear mingled with respect and affection. We revere superiors for their age, their authority, and virtues. We ought to revere parents and upright judges and magistrates. We ought to revere the Lord, His word and His ordinances.

Honor: To revere; to respect; to treat with deference and submission and to perform relative duties to. To treat with due civility and respect in the ordinary intercourse of life. To reverence; manifest the highest veneration for in words and actions; to entertain the most exalted thoughts of. To worship; to adore.

Submit: Having an attitude of wanting to cooperate.

TO RESPECT, HONOR, AND REVERE GOD:

> "With my whole heart have I sought thee: O let me not wander from thy commandments. Thy word have I hid in mine heart, that I might not sin against thee. Blessed art thou, O Lord: teach me thy statutes. With my lips have I declared all the judgments of thy mouth. I have rejoiced in the way of thy testimonies, as much as in all riches. I will meditate in thy precepts, and have respect unto thy ways.

I will delight myself in thy statutes: I will not forget thy word." (Psalm 119:10-16)

God's word is so full of knowledge and understanding, that I have a great respect for it. My respect is not only because of its wisdom, but it also gives us a glimpse of the character and personhood of God. It allows us to know Him in such a way that we as Christians can sense or perceive the existence of this all-powerful, loving, just, invisible, and good, God. When we become born-again, our spirit is born. His greatness, His works, and His creativeness, are made manifest. God is to be revered, honored, and respected above all else.

TO RESPECT, HONOR, REVERE YOUR SPOUSE:

When we submit to our spouse, we yield or surrender to the power, will, and authority of another. We should sometimes sacrifice, or sometimes just yield to their request, even though they may be wrong.

"Submitting yourselves one to another in the fear of God. Wives, submit yourselves unto your own husbands, as unto the Lord. For the husband is the head of the wife, even as Christ is the head of the church: and he is the saviour of the body. Therefore as the church is subject unto Christ, so let the wives be to their own husbands in every thing. Husbands, love your wives, even as Christ also loved the church, and gave himself for it; That he might sanctify and cleanse it with the washing of water by the word, That he might present it to himself a glorious church, not having spot, or wrinkle, or any such thing; but that it should be holy and without blemish. So ought men to love their wives as their own bodies. He that loveth his wife loveth himself. For no man ever yet hated his own flesh; but nourisheth and cherisheth it, even as the Lord the church: For we are members of his body, of his flesh, and of his bones. For this cause shall a man leave his father and mother, and shall be joined unto his wife, and they two shall be one flesh. This is a great mystery: but I speak concerning Christ and the church. Nevertheless let every one of you in particular so love his wife even as himself; and the wife see that she reverence her husband." (Ephesians 5:21-33)

A good example of this submission occurred to me one morning. My wife and I were lying in bed, and she started getting up to go to work. I had the day off and was planning to stay in bed a while longer. She asked me to prepare some coffee for her. I was a little reluctant, but I did so. I sacrificed my bit of rest to make it easier for her. Both husband and wife must have this attitude of respect and sacrifice for one another. The above scriptures are full of concepts of respect of the husband for the wife and the wife for the husband. God's word indicates each has different roles in marriage, and neither is to be treated with less respect. Each is to submit to the other and have an attitude of wanting to cooperate. The wife is to respect her husband as the head of the household. The husband is to honor, respect and love his wife unto death in his protective role. The husband is to love and respect his wife's body as his own and he is to nourish and cherish his wife. The wife is to revere the husband.

TO HONOR, RESPECT YOUR PARENTS:

"Honour thy father and thy mother: that thy days may be long upon the land which the Lord thy God giveth thee." (Exodus 20:12)

It's hard sometimes to honor your parents when you think they're wrong or see their failings. God has called us to honor our parents in spite of their failings or weaknesses. We are all flawed and most parents want the best for their children. Parents and their children are so deeply intertwined genetically, environmentally, morally and emotionally. I am divorced, but have advised my boys to show respect to my ex-wife in spite of my feelings or differences. She is their mother, the one who birthed them, and as with any other person, she has the potential to do great good by fulfilling the purpose God has for her life.

"Children, obey your parents in the Lord: for this is right. Honour thy father and mother; which is the first commandment with promise;" (Ephesians 6:1-2)

Both of my sons have shown great respect for me in different ways. One son has brought his family up in great faith. My other son shows me love in other ways, like his desire to go to the movies with me, and bring me my favorite food (pot pie). They both go to Canada with me. My daughter shows respect in that, although we differ in political views, she is courteous in her differences with me.

TO RESPECT OTHERS:

"Honour all men. Love the brotherhood. Fear God. Honour the king." (1 Peter 2:17)

In all my dealings with others, I believe God calls us to deal respectfully. I believe respect should be benevolent in nature. Benevolent is defined as the disposition to do good; good will; kindness; charitableness; the love of mankind, with the desire to promote their happiness. Of course, there will be those that may take advantage of our benevolence and in this case, boundaries must be set.

TO HONOR AND RESPECT YOUR EMPLOYER:

"Servants, be subject to your masters with all fear; not only to the good and gentle, but also to the froward." (1 Peter 2:18)

More scripture on respect, honor:

"The fear of the Lord is the instruction of wisdom; and before honour is humility." (Proverbs 15:33)

Rest

Rest: Cessation of motion or action of any kind, and applicable to any body or being; rest from labor; rest from mental exertion; rest of body or mind (or emotions); A body is at rest when it ceases to move; the mind (or emotions) are at rest when they cease to be disturbed or agitated; To be quiet or tranquil, as the mind; not to be agitated by fear, anxiety or other passion.

"Rest in the Lord, and wait patiently for him: fret not thyself because of him who prospereth in his way, because of the man who bringeth wicked devices to pass." (Psalm 37:7)

"And on the seventh day God ended his work which he had made; and he rested on the seventh day from all his work which he had made." (Genesis 2:2)

"Six days shalt thou labour, and do all thy work: But the seventh day is the Sabbath of the Lord thy God: in it thou shalt not do any work, thou, nor thy son, nor thy daughter, thy manservant, nor thy maidservant, nor thy cattle, nor thy stranger that is within thy gates: For in six days the Lord made heaven and earth, the sea, and all that in them is, and rested the seventh day: wherefore the Lord blessed the Sabbath day, and hallowed it." (Exodus 20:9-11)

God meant for us to have times of rest. I find rest primarily in three ways; I find rest in my trust of God; I find rest on vacations; I find rest on Sundays, when I do little but worship my God, renewing my mind, body, and emotions. We are to follow God's example, for this is what is best for us. It gives us a chance to slow down and smell the flowers, and to enjoy life. God didn't tell us these things to put a restriction on us, but to show us that this practice is necessary to rest our entire beings.

I believe we can't become too legalistic about this, and say there are no exceptions, because on occasion Jesus healed on the Sabbath. This should be a general rule to follow so as to renew ourselves. If we don't, it could cause us serious health problems. Jesus' life and ministry were very demanding, and His life was busy. To sustain His body, soul, and spirit, He got away from the crowds. He rested and renewed himself by separating himself from the multitudes to have peace, rest, and commune with His Father. We should follow His example.

Other scriptures on rest:

"And straightway Jesus constrained his disciples to go into a ship, and to go before him unto the other side, while he sent the multitude away. And when he had sent the multitude away, he went up into a mountain apart to pray; and when the evening was come, he was there alone." (Matthew 14:22-23)

Selfishness

Selfishness: Loving one's self first.

Self-exaltation: Pride; A conceited sense of one's superiority.

"This know also, that in the last days perilous times shall come. For men shall be lovers of their own selves, covetous, boasters, proud, blasphemers, disobedient to parents, unthankful, unholy." (2 Timothy 3:1-2)

"For all seek their own, not the things which are Jesus Christ's." (Philippians 2:21)

"For thou hast said in thine heart, I will ascend into heaven, I will exalt my throne above the stars of God: I will sit also upon the mount of the congregation, in the sides of the north: I will ascend above the heights of the clouds; I will be like the most High." (Isaiah 14:13-14)

"And the second is like unto it; thou shalt love thy neighbor as thyself." (Matthew 22:39)

Selfishness, self-exaltation, and pride are all found in the devil, the antichrist, and man. The Bible teaches to love our neighbor first, then ourselves. We are to care for the poor, those weaker than ourselves, and look at others as being better than ourselves. I believe most people struggle with selfishness more than any other sin. The antidote to selfishness is self-denial, humility, meekness, and to follow Christ's example.

Other scriptures on selfishness, pride, self-exaltation:

"Let no man deceive you by any means: for that day shall not come, except there come a falling away first, and that man of sin be revealed, the son of perdition; Who opposeth and exalteth himself above all that is called God, or that is worshipped; so that he as God sitteth in the temple of God, shewing himself that he is God." (2 Thessalonians 2:3-4)

Selflessness

Self-denial: The denial of one's self; the forbearing to gratify one's own appetites or desires.

Humility: Freedom from pride and arrogance; humbleness of mind; a modest estimate of one's own worth; In theology, humility consists in lowliness of mind; a deep sense of one's own unworthiness in the sight of God.

> "Teaching us that, denying ungodliness and worldly lusts, we should live soberly, righteously, and godly, in this present world;" (Titus 2:12)

> "The fear of the Lord is the instruction of wisdom; and before honour is humility." (Proverbs 15:33)

A characteristic of someone who is selfless is that they are givers rather than takers. They are self-sacrificing servants. Throughout Christ's ministry, He said He had come to serve. Jesus's washing of the disciple's feet was an example of His servant attitude. Jesus was humble, and meek, of lowly estate. He sacrificed His life for us. No greater love hath a man than to lie down his life for his friends. I, personally, have a deep desire to serve the Lord, to be an example, to spread His word, and to love others as He loved us. I am thankful that the Lord has provided for me. I pray I can be a good steward of what He has given me. I do not have the gift of service, but I can serve in many ways such as facilitating God's word in our prison ministry.

Other scriptures on selflessness, servanthood, humility:

> "And on my servants and on my handmaidens I will pour out in those days of my Spirit; and they shall prophesy:" (Acts 2:18)

> "Likewise, ye younger, submit yourselves unto the elder. Yea, all of you be subject one to another, and be clothed

with humility: for God resisteth the proud, and giveth grace to the humble." (1 Peter 5:5)

"Serving the Lord with all humility of mind, and with many tears, and temptations, which befell me by the lying in wait of the Jews:" (Acts 20:19)

Think

Think: To have the mind occupied on some subject; to have ideas or revolve ideas in the mind. To imagine; to suppose; to fancy. To muse; to meditate. To reflect; to recollect or call to mind. To consider; to deliberate. To conceive. To believe; to esteem.

Thought: That which the mind thinks. Thought is either the act or operation of the mind, when attending to a particular subject or thing it is the idea that is consequent to that operation. We say that a man's thoughts are employed on government, on religion, on trade or arts or his thoughts are employed on his dress or his means of living. By this we mean the mind is directed to that particular subject or object; that is, according to the literal import of the verb think, the mind, the intellectual part of man is set upon such an object, it holds it in view or contemplation, or extends to it, stretches to it.

Imagination: The power of the mind by which it conceives and forms ideas of things communicated to it by the organs of sense. We would define imagination to be the will working on materials of memory; not satisfied by following the order prescribed by nature or suggested by accident, it selects the parts of different conceptions, or objects of memory, to form a whole more pleasing, more terrible, or more awful, than has ever been presented in the ordinary course of nature.

Meditate: To dwell on anything in thought; to study; to turn or revolve any subject in the mind; appropriately but not exclusively used of pious contemplation or a consideration of the great truths of religion.

Contemplation: The act of the mind considering with attention; meditation; study; continuous attention of the mind to a particular subject.

Ponder: To weigh in the mind; to consider and compare circumstances or consequences of an event, or the importance of the reasons for or against a decision.

"And God saw that the wickedness of man was great in the earth, and that every imagination of the thoughts of his heart was only evil continually." (Genesis 6:5)

"Finally, brethren, whatsoever things are true, whatsoever things are honest, whatsoever things are just, whatsoever things are pure, whatsoever things are lovely, whatsoever things are of good report; if there be any virtue, and if there be any praise, think on these things." (Philippians 4:8)

"Casting down imaginations, and every high thing that exalteth itself against the knowledge of God, and bringing into captivity every thought to the obedience of Christ;" (2 Corinthians 10:5)

As with anything else, our thoughts and imaginations can be either good or evil and will dwell on the chosen. I once told my friends I had difficulty with my thought life and I asked for prayer. The scriptures are full of indications that our imaginations and our thoughts are corrupt or evil. It is of necessity that we bring every thought captive to Christ. As we think a wicked thought, we must redirect it to that which is good, and line it up with the goodness of the scriptures. Our thoughts are influenced by what we see, and what our senses bring into our minds. We must think on things that are pure, honest, and good.

I had a friend once tell me that I am a ponderer. I believe this to be true. I am often in thought about what is right or wrong, pondering all the facts regarding a decision. I once read that the majority of people are problem solvers versus goal setters. Being a ponderer, my nature is to be a problem solver. There is a danger to any ponderer/problem solver; the problem is too great and frustration sets in. I have been caught in a loop in solving a problem that I couldn't get out of. But, with God all things are possible. No problem is too great if you call upon God.

I find myself meditating on God's word day and night. As I walk in the morning, as I read the Bible at night, and as I pray often during the day. I meditate on God's word and on my all-powerful, just, loving, merciful, and forgiving God. I think on Jesus's death on the cross for our sins, and I know that I am free and forgiven. I think on God's creation and how wonderful it is, and I find myself feeling joy and peace.

Other scriptures on think, ponder, meditate:

"But Mary kept all these things, and pondered them in her heart." (Luke 2:19)

"Let the words of my mouth, and the meditation of my heart, be acceptable in thy sight, O Lord, my strength, and my redeemer." (Psalm 19:14)

"But his delight is in the law of the Lord; and in his law doth he meditate day and night." (Psalm 1:2)

Trust

Trust: Belief in the honesty, integrity and reliability of another person.

> "It is better to trust in the Lord than to put confidence in man." (Psalm 118:8)

> "Because that, when they knew God, they glorified him not as God, neither were thankful; but became vain in their imaginations, and their foolish heart was darkened. Professing themselves to be wise, they became fools, And changed the glory of the uncorruptible God into an image made like to corruptible man, and to birds, and four-footed beasts, and creeping things. Wherefore God also gave them up to uncleanness through the lusts of their own hearts, to dishonour their own bodies between themselves: Who changed the truth of God into a lie, and worshipped and served the creature more than the Creator, who is blessed for ever. Amen." (Romans 1:21-25)

I believe that trusting a man can be a complicated issue, but it goes without saying that we can trust in God. Can we have that trusting feeling in man? There are basically two categories of men; the saved and the unsaved. The saved, hopefully, are constantly growing in their faith and following God's will...although some are static. Each person is at a different stage of growth. The best we can reach for is being perfect, as Job was. By perfect I mean righteous, a little lower than the angels (Hebrew 2:7, 9). So do we feel trust when dealing with a saved person? Not always. As Christians we make mistakes and sin. All have sinned and fall short of the glory of God. My final conclusion in trusting man is that the godlier a person is – the more trustworthy he is.

Trusting an unsaved person can be complicated too. There are unsaved people who sometimes show more compassion and caring than some that are saved. On the other hand, an unsaved person who continues to expose his mind/soul/heart to evil or wicked influences will in time desensitize himself/herself to evil. There is a danger to the salvation message passing you by too many times. Isaiah 55:6 says, "Seek ye the Lord while he may yet be found, call ye upon him while he is near."

At one point in my life I experienced distrust to the degree that my mind was in torment. I would start out trusting everyone and as time went on there were fewer and fewer people I trusted. At one point I only trusted one person. What a terrible feeling. In my journey, I have pondered deception and misleading someone to believe that which is false or into not believing that which is true. I've pondered motivations, like why they committed an act. Are their motivations good, or evil? In the story of Lazarus and the rich man, the rich man in hell says, "For I have five brethren that he may testify unto them, lest they also come into this place of torment" (Luke 16:28). Hell will be an eternal place of torment. I pray that no one will have to face torment for eternity. Only by a saving faith in Christ can one avoid this end.

Other scriptures on trust:

"For our heart shall rejoice in him, because we have trusted in his holy name." (Psalm 33:21)

"So shall I have wherewith to answer him that reproacheth me: for I trust in thy word." (Psalm 119:42)

Understanding

Understanding: The faculty of the human mind by which it apprehends the real state of things presented to it, or by which it receives or comprehends the ideas which others express and intend to communicate. The understanding is also called the intellectual faculty. It is the faculty by means of which we obtain a great part of knowledge.

"But there is a spirit in man: and the inspiration of the Almighty giveth them understanding." (Job 32:8)

"And the spirit of the Lord shall rest upon him, the spirit of wisdom and understanding, the spirit of counsel and might, the spirit of knowledge and of the fear of the Lord; And shall make him of quick understanding in the fear of the Lord: and he shall not judge after the sight of his eyes, neither reprove after the hearing of his ears:" (Isaiah 11:2-3)

"Give therefore thy servant an understanding heart to judge thy people, that I may discern between good and bad: for who is able to judge this thy so great a people? And the speech pleased the Lord, that Solomon had asked this thing. And God said unto him, Because thou hast asked this thing, and hast not asked for thyself long life; neither hast asked riches for thyself, nor hast asked the life of thine enemies; but hast asked for thyself understanding to discern judgment; Behold, I have done according to thy words: lo, I have given thee a wise and an understanding heart; so that there was none like thee before thee, neither after thee shall any arise like unto thee." (1 Kings 3:9-12)

I have asked the Lord for a wise and understanding heart, a spirit of wisdom and understanding, and a spirit of counsel. My intent is to use my life experiences and my gifting; prophecy, mercy, and encouragement – combined with the counseling I have heard, to counsel others who have had similar experiences. I await this gifting with great anticipation and hope, that I may fulfill God's purpose in my life.

Perverted understanding: Understanding turned from right to wrong; distorted; corrupted; misinterpretation; misemployed.

"All scripture is given by inspiration of God, and is profitable for doctrine, for reproof, for correction, for instruction in righteousness: That the man of God may be perfect, thoroughly furnished unto all good works." (2 Timothy 3:16-17)

I heard a pastor who gave a sermon regarding his beliefs on the Bible and what Jesus said. He said that unless Jesus said it in the Bible it wasn't true. Immediately I could sense this was wrong. It gave me an uneasy, unsettled feeling. The pastor selectively chose what he wanted to believe. This is not uncommon. Currently there is a homosexual pastor about to be ordained as a minister in the Episcopal Church. When he is asked how he reconciles scriptures on Sodom and Gomorrah and homosexuality (men lying with men and women lying with women) being an abomination unto the Lord, he says God is love and this overrides everything else. Once again, he is being selective in what he wants to believe in the Bible; in this case to justify his sin. God is also holy, righteous, and just, which negates his argument that God is OK with homosexuality.

When a person selectively chooses only a portion of scripture and that becomes their doctrinal understanding, they have set themselves up as gods. Genesis 3:4-5 says, "And the serpent said unto the woman ye shall surely not die: for God doth know that the day that you eat thereof, then your eyes will be opened, and ye shall be as gods, knowing good and evil." **All** scripture is given by the inspiration of God, and to selectively choose what you will and will not believe in the Bible will end up disastrous.

Other scriptures on understanding:

"He hath blinded their eyes, and hardened their heart; that they should not see with their eyes, nor understand with their heart, and be converted, and I should heal them." (John 12:40)

"Now I am come to make thee understand what shall befall thy people in the latter days: for yet the vision is for many days." (Daniel 10:14)

Vision

Vision: In scripture, a revelation from God; an appearance or exhibition of something supernaturally presented to the minds of prophets, by which they were informed of future events. Such were the visions of Isaiah, of Amos, of Ezekiel and company.

Dream: The thought or a series of thoughts of a person in sleep. We apply dream in the singular, to a series of thoughts, which occupy the mind of a sleeping person, in which he imagines he has a view of real things or transactions. A dream is a series of thoughts not under the command of reason, and hence wild and irregular. In scripture, dreams were sometimes impressions on the minds of sleeping persons, made by divine agency. God came to Abimelech in a dream. Joseph was warned by God in a dream.

"Where there is no vision, the people perish: but he that keepeth the law, happy is he." (Proverbs 29:18)

VISIONS:
It is in my heart that the mentally ill and the broken-hearted be healed, and as much as possible, that breakdowns such as mine be avoided. I said to a Christian Psychologist, that Christian Psychologists, Psychiatrists, and those non-Christian Psychologists and Psychiatrists with caring hearts have been waging the war against mental illness alone for some time. It's time that the full ranks of the church join the battle.

Matthew 16:18 says, "And I say also unto thee, that thou art Peter, and upon this rock I will build my church; and the gates of hell will not prevail against it. The song "Onward Christian Soldiers" comes to mind. The church is currently in the battle and many are doing several things well. But no man has all truth and no church has all truth. We the church must increase our efforts, or lose many Christians as well as non-Christians to mental illness.

I view the following as necessary steps in this battle: increased prayer; increased counseling, perhaps qualified people in lay ministry such as the Stephens Ministry. Through this ministry, establish a communication network across the country sharing information about mental illness (not names) and how to combat it (the church must become smart about how to share this information so as not to violate privacy laws). Are there lawyers in the church? I believe the church must be a place of rest, peace, refuge, and healing. I also believe that the church should fund scholarships to Christian colleges to increase the number of Christian Psychologists and Psychiatrists. There are far too few in existence in this country.

DREAMS:
On January 8, 1996, I had a wonderful dream. I dreamt I went to heaven. While there, Jesus said to me, "You've done good things and bad things". For a moment I felt sad. But then I felt an overwhelming feeling of forgiveness and I heard Jesus interceding for me, saying "most of the time he just didn't know." Then He said, "all those things you didn't understand, I'm going to explain to you now." He said there would no longer be any tears, pain or suffering for me. "And all the bad people that hurt you on earth, won't be able to hurt you anymore because they won't be up here in heaven." He also said "you know those good things you did? I was oh, so proud of you." Then I remember hearing the song "When we all get to heaven, oh how happy we will be. When we all see Jesus, we will sing and shout the victory."

Perhaps this is a dream as indicated in Joel 2:28. It says, "And afterward I will pour out my Spirit on all people. Your sons and daughters will prophesy, your old men will dream dreams and young men will see visions. 2 Corinthians 5:10 says, "for we must all appear before the judgment seat of

Christ; that every one may receive the things done in this body, according to that he hath done, whether it be good or bad."

Other scriptures on dreams:

"And Joseph dreamed a dream, and he told it his brethren: and they hated him yet the more. And he said unto them, Hear, I pray you, this dream which I have dreamed: For, behold, we were binding sheaves in the field, and, lo, my sheaf arose, and also stood upright; and, behold, your sheaves stood round about, and made obeisance to my sheaf. And his brethren said to him, Shalt thou indeed reign over us? or shalt thou indeed have dominion over us? And they hated him yet the more for his dreams, and for his words. And he dreamed yet another dream, and told it his brethren, and said, Behold, I have dreamed a dream more; and, behold, the sun and the moon and the eleven stars made obeisance to me. And he told it to his father, and to his brethren: and his father rebuked him, and said unto him, What is this dream that thou hast dreamed? Shall I and thy mother and thy brethren indeed come to bow down ourselves to thee to the earth?" (Genesis 37:5-10)

Will

Will: That faculty of the mind by which we determine to do or forbear (stop; cease from doing) an action; the faculty which is exercised in deciding, among two or more objects, which we will embrace or pursue. The will is directed or influenced by judgment. The understanding or reason compares different objects, which operate as motives; the judgment determines which is preferable, and the will decides which to pursue. In other words, we reason with respect to the value or importance of things; we then judge which is preferable and we will to take the most valuable. These are but different operations of the mind, soul or intellectual part of man. Great disputes have existed respecting the freedom of will. Choice; determination; Command; direction; Our prayers should be according to the will of God. To determine; to decide in the mind that something shall be done or forborne; implying power to carry the purpose into effect.

Purpose: That which a person sets before himself as an object to be reached or accomplished. The end or aim to which the view is directed in any plan, measure or exertion.

OBEDIENT VS. DISOBEDIENT:
Obedient: Compliant with a command, prohibition or known rule of duty prescribed; the performance of what is enjoined by authority or the abstaining from what is prohibited. To constitute obedience, the act or forbearance to act must be in submission to authority; the command must be known to the person and his compliance must be in consequence of it, or it is not obedience. Obedience which duty requires, implies dignity of conduct rather than servility. Obedience may be voluntary or involuntary. Voluntary obedience alone can be acceptable to God. Government must compel the obedience of individuals; otherwise who will seek its protection or fear its vengeance?

Disobedient: Neglect or refusal to obey; omitting to do what is commanded or doing what is prohibited; not observant of duty or rules prescribed by authority e.g. children disobedient to parents, citizens disobedient to laws, people disobedient to God's laws.

"I call heaven and earth to record this day against you, that I have set before you life and death, blessing and cursing: therefore choose life, that both thou and thy seed may live:" (Deuteronomy 30:19)

"And if it seem evil unto you to serve the Lord, choose you this day whom ye will serve; whether the gods which your fathers served that were on the other side of the flood, or the gods of the Amorites, in whose land ye dwell: but as for me and my house, we will serve the Lord." (Joshua 24:15)

"If ye be willing and obedient, ye shall eat the good of the land:" (Isaiah 1:19)

"If ye keep my commandments, ye shall abide in my love; even as I have kept my Father's commandments, and abide in his love." (John 15:10)

"Blessed are they that do his commandments, that they may have right to the tree of life, and may enter in through the gates into the city." (Revelation 22:14)

"But if thou shalt indeed obey his voice, and do all that I speak; then I will be an enemy unto thine enemies, and an adversary unto thine adversaries." (Exodus 23:22)

"If ye walk in my statutes, and keep my commandments, and do them, then I will give you rain in due season, and the land shall yield her increase, and the trees of the field shall yield their fruit." (Leviticus 26:3-4)

"And I will give peace in the land, and ye shall lie down, and none shall make you afraid: and I will rid evil beasts out of the land, neither shall the sword go through your land." (Leviticus 26:6)

DISOBEDIENCE:

I believe some of the clearest and most frightening consequences of disobedience can be found in Deuteronomy 28:15-65: God's word says people/nations will be cursed. The verb curse is defined as to injure; to subject to evil; to vex (trouble, harass or torment with great calamities). Here are some of the verses:

> "But it shall come to pass, if thou wilt not hearken unto the voice of the Lord thy God, to observe to do all his commandments and his statutes which I command thee this day; that all these curses shall come upon thee, and overtake thee: Cursed shalt thou be in the city, and cursed shalt thou be in the field. Cursed shall be thy basket and thy store. Cursed shall be the fruit of thy body, and the fruit of thy land, the increase of thy kine, and the flocks of thy sheep. Cursed shalt thou be when thou comest in, and cursed shalt thou be when thou goest out. The Lord shall send upon thee cursing, vexation, and rebuke, in all that thou settest thine hand unto for to do, until thou be destroyed, and until thou perish quickly; because of the wickedness of thy doings, whereby thou hast forsaken me." (Deuteronomy 28:15-20)

> "For as by one man's disobedience many were made sinners, so by the obedience of one shall many be made righteous." (Romans 5:19)

The scriptures say that God gives us free will to choose between good and evil, to be obedient or disobedient. Men or women may try to usurp our free will unjustly, but God will not usurp our free will. We may choose life or death, blessing or cursing, good or evil. God's word urges us to strongly consider whether we will choose His way or the world's way. He urges us to choose life. When we use our will to be obedient, or to follow God's will, there are definite benefits. I pray that all will choose obedience to God over disobedience, for the earthly consequences of disobedience are harsh but the eternal consequences are too terrible to imagine, or bear.

Other scriptures on obedience/disobedience:

"For if we sin wilfully after that we have received the knowledge of the truth, there remaineth no more sacrifice for sins, But a certain fearful looking for of judgment and fiery indignation, which shall devour the adversaries." (Hebrews 10:26-27)

"And if thou wilt walk in my ways, to keep my statutes and my commandments, as thy father David did walk, then I will lengthen thy days." (1 Kings 3:14)

"But whoso hearkeneth unto me shall dwell safely, and shall be quiet from fear of evil." (Proverbs 1:33)

Spiritual Birth

Birth: The act of coming to life or of being born.

Born: To be born or born again is to be regenerated, renewed; to receive spiritual life.

> "Jesus answered and said unto him, Verily, verily, I say unto thee, Except a man be born again, he cannot see the kingdom of God." (John 3:3)

> "Therefore if any man be in Christ, he is a new creature: old things are passed away; behold, all things are become new." (2 Corinthians 5:17)

To be born-again is to have a consciousness that there is an omnipotent (all-powerful), loving, merciful, just God that truly exists, cares about us, knows us inside and out, and protects us. My spiritual birth occurred during or shortly after a counseling session. I felt evil was all around me, and it was greater than I thought I could bear. The counselor said to me "God would be insulted if you thought evil was greater than Him." That started me thinking that there really is a being that exists, that is greater than all evil. This started my God consciousness.

I knew there was a God. I had a clear and certain perception that God exists. I knew there was an all-powerful God watching over me. That's not to say I wouldn't have some fear in the future, but as I grew in Christ, I began to trust Him more and more in my life. I still had problems but I knew God was there to depend on, and to help me through my troubles.

Other scriptures on spiritual birth:

"Jesus answered, Verily, verily, I say unto thee, Except a man be born of water and of the Spirit, he cannot enter into the kingdom of God. That which is born of the flesh is flesh; and that which is born of the Spirit is spirit. Marvel not that I said unto thee, Ye must be born again. The wind bloweth where it listeth, and thou hearest the sound thereof, but canst not tell whence it cometh, and whither it goeth: so is every one that is born of the Spirit." (John 3:5-8)

"Being born again, not of corruptible seed, but of incorruptible, by the word of God, which liveth and abideth for ever." (1 Peter 1:23)

"Whosoever is born of God doth not commit sin; for his seed remaineth in him: and he cannot sin, because he is born of God. In this the children of God are manifest, and the children of the devil: whosoever doeth not righteousness is not of God, neither he that loveth not his brother." (1 John 3:9-10)

Critical Spirit

Critical: Relating to criticism; inclined to find fault or judge with severity.

Fault: Properly, an erring, or missing; a failure; hence an error or mistake; a blunder; a defect; a blemish; whatever impairs excellence. In morals, any error or defect; an imperfection; any deviation from propriety; a slight offense; Fault implies wrong and some degree of criminality.

To find fault: To express blame; to complain.

Judge: Criticize

Murmur: To grumble; complain; to utter sullen discontent.

> "And Levi made him a great feast in his own house: and there was a great company of publicans and of others that sat down with them. But their scribes and Pharisees murmured against his disciples, saying, Why do ye eat and drink with publicans and sinners? And Jesus answering said unto them, They that are whole need not a physician; but they that are sick. I came not to call the righteous, but sinners to repentance." (Luke 5:29-32)

> "Then took Mary a pound of ointment of spikenard, very costly, and anointed the feet of Jesus, and wiped his feet with her hair: and the house was filled with the odour of the ointment. Then saith one of his disciples, Judas Iscariot, Simon's son, which should betray him, Why was not this ointment sold for three hundred pence, and given to the poor? This he said, not that he cared for the poor; but because he was a thief, and had the bag, and bare what was put therein. Then said Jesus, Let her alone: against the day of my burying hath she kept this. For the poor always ye have with you; but me ye have not always." (John 12:3-8)

"And Miriam and Aaron spake against Moses because of the Ethiopian woman whom he had married: for he had married an Ethiopian woman." (Numbers 12:1)

"And the anger of the Lord was kindled against them; and he departed. And the cloud departed from off the tabernacle; and, behold, Miriam became leprous, white as snow: and Aaron looked upon Miriam, and, behold, she was leprous." (Numbers 12:1)

In the above scriptures, there are three examples of critical spirits. The Pharisees criticized the disciples; Judas Iscariot found fault with Mary for putting ointment on Jesus' feet; and Miriam found fault with Moses, one of God's anointed prophets. In each case, Jesus or God came to the defense of those criticized. Jesus/God was angry, and not pleased with their criticism and rebuked them; and in Miriam's case, struck her with leprosy. It can be very dangerous to criticize God's anointed. To be overly critical of our spouse or anyone is wrong. How do we decide what is being overly critical? Often, we mean only to constructively criticize or teach someone what is right. Once again, too much criticism or fault finding will tear down a person and bring pain to the mind and emotions of the recipient.

Other scriptures on criticism:

"But when the Pharisees saw it, they said unto him, Behold, thy disciples do that which is not lawful to do upon the sabbath day." (Matthew 12:2)

"Then came to Jesus scribes and Pharisees, which were of Jerusalem, saying, Why do thy disciples transgress the tradition of the elders? for they wash not their hands when they eat bread." (Matthew 12:1-2)

"Or how wilt thou say to thy brother, Let me pull out the mote out of thine eye; and, behold, a beam is in thine own eye?" (Matthew 7:4)

Fruit of the Spirit
Love

Love: To have benevolence or good will toward.

Benevolent: Having a disposition to do good, possessing love to mankind, and a desire to promote their prosperity and happiness; kind.

Charity: In general sense, love, benevolence, good will; that disposition of the heart which inclines men to think favorably of their fellow man and to do them good. In a theological sense, it includes supreme love to God, and universal good will to men.

> "And the second is like, namely this, Thou shalt love thy neighbour as thyself. There is none other commandment greater than these." (Mark 12:31)

> "And now abideth faith, hope, charity, these three; but the greatest of these is charity." (1 Corinthians 13:13)

> "But I say unto you, Love your enemies, bless them that curse you, do good to them that hate you, and pray for them which despitefully use you, and persecute you;" (Matthew 5:44)

Love is an action as well as a feeling. When someone does an act of love to you, you feel loved. There are seven types of love: God's supernatural love, agape (among primitive Christians, a love fest or feast of charity love), brotherly love, Eros love (physical love between a man and a woman), unconditional (Absolute; unreserved; not limited by any conditions), Conditional (a limited).

LOVED BY OTHERS:
When I was about seven, and my brother was ten, he protected me from being beaten up by a bully. Recently, when I

was close to a breakdown, because of my diabetes, my wife and my daughter tried to have me committed. They did not know that it was not my bipolar problem, but that it was the diabetes which had the same symptoms. I say this because my big brother came to my defense again. His love for me is great and he felt he was protecting someone weaker than him, which is biblical (Psalm 82:3). His feelings of protection are so strong that he still hasn't gotten over it, but I'm sure in time he will.

LOVE OF MY PARENTS:
I believe my parents were one of my greatest blessings from God. They have truly been a good example to follow. My mom was a very special person. She cared deeply about her family and was a godly woman. In her earlier years, she could have been a beauty queen. In her later years, her beauty was in terms of her courage as she faced each day with pain and complained little. She suffered with arthritis, hip, back and foot pain, and diabetes. My father was the same way. He had 21 operations, had his nose removed and replaced via surgery, but complained little. He was an adventurer and had a dry wit about him.

My fondest memories of my mom were as she served me cocoa and toast each morning for breakfast. She always got me my favorite foods, like pork roll, Lipton's noodle soup, macaroni and cheese, pot pie, and meatloaf. My fondest memories of my father were on our adventures together. We once went canoeing on the Susquehanna. We had a motor on the canoe but the pin was sheered, and we had to paddle. A storm came up quickly and the waves were two feet high. My father told us to paddle into the waves and we made it back safely. Another time, I fell through the ice while ice skating and he saved my life by pulling me out quickly.

LOVE OF MY SPOUSE:
Ephesians 5:25 says, "Husbands love your wives even as Christ also loved the church and gave Himself for it". My wife

and I fell in love, and after our wedding went on our honeymoon to Virginia Beach, Virginia. While there, we were able to get on the 700 Club show with Pat Robertson. We had a great time. My wife's heart's desire was to have a child. She was infertile so we had to adopt. She struggled deeply with this issue. The more we got into the process, the more they wanted to know about us. I don't believe they left many issues unturned, including my bipolar illness. As they began to ask questions, a great fear/shame began to develop in me. I believe there is a fear in man to expose all that he is because of all his sins and weaknesses. Mine, of course, was magnified because of my mental illness.

I struggled with the questions, with the fear, and I believe the adoption process to be the hardest thing I have ever done. I had to go beyond my fears and give my wife her heart's desire. I believe my wife sensed some of my struggle, but not the severity of it. I overcame my fear but realized how weak I am as a man without the Lord's help. I had prayed for strength on a number of occasions and I got through it. I can do all things through Christ, which strengthens me (Philippians 4:13). The rewards have been great as a result of this adoption, but it has not been without its struggles. I love my daughter deeply, and she returns that love in ways I could not have imagined. She makes me feel ten feet tall.

LOVE OF MY CHILDREN AND GRANDCHILDREN:
All are very dear to me. I love giving to them on Christmas and birthdays. They all have special gifts and personalities. One has the gift of leadership, another one of mercy. Each has shown great concern in my times of troubles. I am proud of them all and couldn't have asked for better children and grandchildren.

LOVE OF OTHERS:
We are to love others as ourselves and even count others better than ourselves. We are to love our enemies and pray for

them. We are to pray for those who persecute us. There's a song by Michael W. Smith called "Friends." It says "Friends are friends forever if the Lord's the Lord of them." The more godly a friend, the more you can depend on them to treat you well, and help you in times of need, being a blessing to you and your family.

Other scriptures on love:

"There is no fear in love; but perfect love casteth out fear: because fear hath torment. He that feareth is not made perfect in love." (1 John 4:18)

"Be of the same mind one toward another. Mind not high things, but condescend to men of low estate. Be not wise in your own conceits." (Romans 12:16)

"And it came to pass afterward, that he loved a woman in the valley of Sorek, whose name was Delilah." (Judges 16:4)

"And she said unto him, How canst thou say, I love thee, when thine heart is not with me? thou hast mocked me these three times, and hast not told me wherein thy great strength lieth." (Judges 16:15)

"Defend the poor and fatherless: do justice to the afflicted and needy. Deliver the poor and needy: rid them out of the hand of the wicked." (Psalm 82:3-4)

"But I say unto you, Love your enemies, bless them that curse you, do good to them that hate you, and pray for them which despitefully use you, and persecute you;" (Matthew 5:44)

"Bless them that curse you, and pray for them which despitefully use you." (Luke 6:28)

"And as ye would that men should do to you, do ye also to them likewise." (Luke 6:31)

In case you didn't notice, Luke 6:31 is The Golden Rule.

Fruit of the Spirit
Joy

Joy: The passion or emotion excited by the acquisition or expectation of good; that excitement of pleasurable feelings which is caused by success, good fortune, the gratification of desire or some good possessed; or by a rational prospect of possessing what we love or desire; gladness or exultation.

Happy: Being in the enjoyment of agreeable sensations from the possession of good; enjoying pleasure from the gratification of appetites or desires (This renders a person temporarily happy); but he is only permanently happy who enjoys peace of mind in the favor of God. To be in any degree happy we must be free from pain both of body and mind.

Blessed: Happy; prosperous in worldly affairs; enjoying heavenly felicity (great happiness).

"Then he said unto them, Go your way, eat the fat, and drink the sweet, and send portions unto them for whom nothing is prepared: for this day is holy unto our Lord: neither be ye sorry; for the joy of the Lord is your strength." (Nehemiah 8:10)

"Thou wilt shew me the path of life: in thy presence is fullness of joy; at thy right hand there are pleasures for evermore." (Psalm 16:11)

"My brethren, count it all joy when ye fall into divers temptations; Knowing this, that the trying of your faith worketh patience. But let patience have her perfect work, that ye may be perfect and entire, wanting nothing." (James 1:2-4)

"How that in a great trial of affliction the abundance of their joy and their deep poverty abounded unto the riches of their liberality." (2 Corinthians 8:2)

God and God's word give me the greatest joy, but I'm still on Earth and there are a lot of things that bring me joy. (1) art; my favorite paintings are *Gone with the Wind* by Thomas Kinkade, *Peace* by Harmony Glazer, *Jesus Wept* by Erik Hollandér, *Well Done* by Jerry Anderson, *Leapfrog* by Norman Rockwell, *Adam in the Garden of Eden* by Tom Debois, and *Daniel in the Lion's Den* by H. Autes; (2) fishing; my favorite fishing is in Ontario. I've been going to Canada for 53 years; (3) my family; my mom, my dad, my brother, my sister, my daughter, my two sons, and my five grandchildren; (4) movies; my favorite movies are *Friendly Persuasion* with Gary Cooper, *I Bought a Zoo* with Matt Damon, *Big Jake* and *Chisum* with John Wayne, *Ben-Hur*, *Simon Birch*, *The Ten Commandments*, and *The Bible*; (5) animals; animals have brought me joy – dogs, cats, a raccoon, squirrel, rabbits, and tropical fish; (6) godly music; "Breath of Heaven" by Amy Grant, "It's a Wonderful World" by Louie Armstrong, "Friends" by Michael W. Smith, "You Can Only Imagine" by Bart Millard, "Mary Did You Know" by Mark Lowry, "The Love of God, Prince of Peace" by Marty Goetzand; (7) books; "This Present Darkness," "Piercing the Darkness" by Frank Peretti, "Left Behind" series by Tim Lahaye, "Final Dawn Over Jerusalem" by John Hagee, and "The Late Great Planet Earth" by Hal Lindsey.

Comment: My daughter reads over a thousand pages a day. Within a short time, she had read every book in our house. She is planning to go to college so she can become a librarian. My son is an environmental scientist cleaning up the streams in western Pennsylvania. My other son is third in command at a large restaurant. I'm so proud of all my children, and they bring me so much joy.

Other Scriptures on Joy:

"Sing unto him a new song; play skilfully with a loud noise." (Psalm 33:3)

"Praise him with the sound of the trumpet: praise him with the psaltery and harp." (Psalm 150:3)

"What is it then? I will pray with the spirit, and I will pray with the understanding also: I will sing with the spirit, and I will sing with the understanding also." (1 Corinthians 14:15)

"Blessed is the nation whose God is the Lord; and the people whom he hath chosen for his own inheritance." (Psalm 33:12)

"Happy is the man that findeth wisdom, and the man that getteth understanding." (Proverbs 3:13)

"Blessed is he whose transgression is forgiven, whose sin is covered." (Psalm 32:1)

Fruit of the Spirit
Peace

Peace: In a general sense, a state of quiet or tranquility; freedom from disturbance or agitation by the passions as from fear, terror, anger, anxiety or the like (jealousy, envy, pride, grief); quietness of mind, tranquility, calmness, quiet of conscience; heavenly rest.

"Thou hast dealt well with thy servant, O Lord, according unto thy word." (Psalm 119:65)

"The Lord bless thee, and keep thee: The Lord make his face shine upon thee, and be gracious unto thee: The Lord lift up his countenance upon thee, and give thee peace." (Numbers 6: 24-26)

"The Lord will give strength unto his people; the Lord will bless his people with peace." (Psalm 29:11)

One thing that brings me great peace, especially when I'm troubled, is godly music. Songs like "God Will Make a Way," and other worship songs. There was a time when my heart was in turmoil and a godly song brought back the calmness to my spirit, and lifted my spirits. The words in the songs must be words of life to be of great benefit, such as those from the scriptures. I thank God for our godly musicians who have blessed my life this way.

I have experienced the peace, tranquility, and calmness of the mind as I sat quietly near our tropical fish/goldfish watching them swim back and forth in our aquarium. During these quiet, calm times I feel very blessed and thank God I can experience such peace. Peace is also spiritual rest. I began to read scriptures on peace and thought, perhaps I should analyze what brings about spiritual rest from God's word. But I came to the conclusion that God just wanted me to rest in his word. As I read the following scriptures, I had a great peace and prayed this peace would come on our home.

"When he giveth quietness, who then can make trouble? and when he hideth his face, who then can behold him? whether it be done against a nation, or against a man only:" (Job 34:29)

"I will both lay me down in peace, and sleep: for thou, Lord, only makest me dwell in safety." (Psalm 4:8)

"What man is he that feareth the Lord? him shall he teach in the way that he shall choose." (Psalm 25:12)

"Thou wilt keep him in perfect peace, whose mind is stayed on thee: because he trusteth in thee." (Isaiah 26:3)

"O that thou hadst hearkened to my commandments! then had thy peace been as a river, and thy righteousness as the waves of the sea:" (Isaiah 48:18)

"Let our lord now command thy servants, which are before thee, to seek out a man, who is a cunning player on an harp: and it shall come to pass, when the evil spirit from God is upon thee, that he shall play with his hand, and thou shalt be well." (1 Samuel 16:16)

Fruit of the Spirit
Patience

Patience: Undergoing pain or suffering without losing your self-control or complaining; the act or quality of waiting long for justice or expected good without discontent; the quality of bearing offenses or injustices without anger or revenge.

Long-suffering: Bearing injuries or provocation for a long time; patient; not easily provoked.

Wait: To stay or rest in expectation; to stop or remain stationary, until the arrival of some person or event.

> "And the Lord passed by before him, and proclaimed, The Lord, The Lord God, merciful and gracious, longsuffering, and abundant in goodness and truth," (Exodus 34:6)

> "And not only so, but we glory in tribulations also: knowing that tribulation worketh patience; And patience, experience; and experience, hope:" (Romans 5:3-4)

God is doing a work in my wife, Robin, and me, to develop patience in us. Here is a situation where my wife must endure and, because we are one, I must also. My wife has over 50 allergies (which could easily turn into an asthma attack.) They wear her down constantly. Her allergies range not only from trees, grass, bushes, cats, dogs, and molds, but to many types of food, such as, dyes, onions, etc. Her nose is often clogged and many times she cannot sleep. She is up as many as three or four times a night. We have called upon the Lord to set her free of these allergies but no answer has come.

This affects me in many ways, too. I am extremely sensitive to noise. Her allergies are alleviated by air cleaners, which are noisy. We have many. When she awakes at night, I am often awakened. We have spent significant amounts of money for medical treatments, air cleaners, and the best of all air filters for the air conditioner. My parents and sons have cats, which limit the time we can spend with them. When we come back from a visit, we must all shower immediately to get off the cat dander. In a sense, we've had a small taste of hell and torment.

Robin is as careful as she can be about her health and has done her part. Few people can fully understand the depth of suffering she experiences when exposed to allergens and the precautions she must take to safeguard her health. My wife often talks about the safeguards she must take, and when I don't feel good, it's hard to listen. Robin is the real hero in terms of patience, although I must also endure as a result of her allergies.

Other scriptures on patience, long-suffering, waiting:

"My brethren, count it all joy when ye fall into divers temptations; Knowing this, that the trying of your faith worketh patience. But let patience have her perfect work, that ye may be perfect and entire, wanting nothing." (Romans 5:3-4)

"Behold, we count them happy which endure. Ye have heard of the patience of Job, and have seen the end of the Lord; that the Lord is very pitiful, and of tender mercy." (James 5:11)

"Our soul waiteth for the Lord: he is our help and our shield." (Psalm 33:20)

"I waited patiently for the Lord; and he inclined unto me, and heard my cry." (Psalm 40:1)

Fruit of the Spirit
Kindness

Kindness: Good will; benevolence; that temper or disposition which delights in the contributing to the happiness of others, which is exercised cheerfully in gratifying their wishes, supplying their wants or alleviating their distresses. Kindness consists of five elements, i.e. friendliness, generosity, sympathy, gentleness, and tender-heartedness.

Mercy: Kindness in excess of what is fair. That benevolence, mildness or tenderness of heart which disposes a person to overlook injuries or treat an offender better that he deserves; the disposition that tempers justice and induces an injured person to forgive trespasses and injuries, and to forbear punishment, or inflict less than law or justice will warrant. In this sense, there is no word precisely synonymous with mercy. That which comes closest to it is grace.

> "O give thanks unto the Lord; for he is good: for his mercy endureth for ever. O give thanks unto the God of gods: for his mercy endureth for ever. O give thanks to the Lord of lords: for his mercy endureth for ever. To him who alone doeth great wonders: for his mercy endureth for ever. To him that by wisdom made the heavens: for his mercy endureth for ever. To him that stretched out the earth above the waters: for his mercy endureth for ever. To him that made great lights: for his mercy endureth for ever: The sun to rule by day: for his mercy endureth for ever: The moon and stars to rule by night: for his mercy endureth for ever. To him that smote Egypt in their first-born: for his mercy endureth for ever: And brought out Israel from among them: for his mercy endureth for ever: With a strong hand, and with a stretched out arm: for his mercy endureth for ever. To him which divided the Red sea into parts: for his mercy endureth for ever: And

made Israel to pass through the midst of it: for his mercy endureth for ever: But overthrew Pharaoh and his host in the Red sea: for his mercy endureth for ever. To him which led his people through the wilderness: for his mercy endureth for ever. To him which smote great kings: for his mercy endureth for ever: And slew famous kings: for his mercy endureth for ever: Sihon king of the Amorites: for his mercy endureth for ever: And Og the king of Bashan: for his mercy endureth for ever: And gave their land for an heritage: for his mercy endureth for ever: Even an heritage unto Israel his servant: for his mercy endureth for ever. Who remembered us in our low estate: for his mercy endureth for ever: And hath redeemed us from our enemies: for his mercy endureth for ever. Who giveth food to all flesh: for his mercy endureth for ever. O give thanks unto the God of heaven: for his mercy endureth for ever." (Psalm 136:1-26)

Psalm 136 states "for His mercy endureth forever" twenty six times. Over the years I have witnessed to my sister and brother-in-law, sometimes very clumsily. They were both very gracious in not expressing any offense to me. There was a question in my heart as to the status of their salvation. I didn't see many fruits yet, though my sister confessed her faith in Christ in a letter to a previous pastor of mine.

When my sister was in her forties, she fell and was severely injured, and went into a coma. I struggled with my sister's salvation and what her eternal destination might be. I prayed and read to her Psalm 136 many times while she was in the coma. I called upon God's mercy that her soul might be saved. I also sought counsel on this issue and what I should recommend to my brother-in-law about turning off the machines that were keeping her alive. The pastor that counseled me was previously an undertaker and was well familiar with issues on death. He said to me "Is it man prolonging her life or God?" He said it may be time to let her go. When my brother-in-law decided to let the doctors turn off the machines, I did not object. I believe my brother-in-law made the right decision.

Regarding salvation, I'm not sure anyone can fully know the depth and breadth of God's mercy or whether some day he will pass down judgment on us. When it's my time to be with the Lord, I hope to see my sister in heaven. Psalm 136 has become precious to me because of this experience.

During the height of my mental illness, I was not very productive at work. My employer was merciful and kept me on, for which I am very grateful for both me and my family.

Other scriptures on kindness and mercy.

"Blessed are the merciful: for they shall obtain mercy." (Matthew 5:7)

"It is of the Lord's mercies that we are not consumed, because his compassions fail not. They are new every morning: great is thy faithfulness." (Lamentations 3:22-23)

"Charity suffereth long, and is kind; charity envieth not; charity vaunteth not itself, is not puffed up," (1 Corinthians 13:4)

"And be ye kind one to another, tenderhearted, forgiving one another, even as God for Christ's sake hath forgiven you." (Ephesians 4:32)

Fruit of the Spirit
Goodness

Goodness: The moral qualities which constitute Christian excellence; moral virtue; kindness; benevolence; a generous heart; acts of kindness, charity, and humanity exercised.

> "Finally, brethren, whatsoever things are true, whatsoever things are honest, whatsoever things are just, whatsoever things are pure, whatsoever things are lovely, whatsoever things are of good report; if there be any virtue, and if there be any praise, think on these things." (Philippians 4:8)

When we do acts of goodness, there are good, pleasant, cheerful, happy, satisfied feelings generated if the person(s) are open and capable of those feelings. I have experienced much goodness in my life. I've told my parents that I consider them to be one of God's greatest blessings to me. I consider my in-laws to be a second set of parents to me. My wife is good to me in spite of my flaws. I have two good boys. My daughter makes me feel ten feet tall.

In comparison to many in the world, I would be considered to have abundant wealth: a good home; two good cars; and a good job. I go to a good church that lifts me up. I have good memories of my childhood and my grandparents. Have you ever had a pea shooter battle and the next year pea plants were growing everywhere? We did, at my grandparents. It still brings a smile to my face when I think of it. My dad took us on canoe trips on the Susquehanna River and in Canada. Our family often went to the woodlands to camp as my father owned 30 acres in York County. The list could go on and on. All of these good things leave me with a pleasant feeling.

Other scriptures on goodness:

"I know that there is no good in them, but for a man to rejoice, and to do good in his life. And also that every man should eat and drink, and enjoy the good of all his labour, it is the gift of God." (Ecclesiastes 3:12-13)

"The Lord is good unto them that wait for him, to the soul that seeketh him. It is good that a man should both hope and quietly wait for the salvation of the Lord." (Lamentations 3:25-26)

"Withhold not good from them to whom it is due, when it is in the power of thine hand to do it." (Proverbs 3:27)

"Evil pursueth sinners: but to the righteous good shall be repayed." (Proverbs 13:21)

"How God anointed Jesus of Nazareth with the Holy Ghost and with power: who went about doing good, and healing all that were oppressed of the devil; for God was with him." (Acts 10:38)

"But glory, honour, and peace, to every man that worketh good, to the Jew first, and also to the Gentile:" (Romans 2:10)

"I am the good shepherd: the good shepherd giveth his life for the sheep." (John 10:11)

Fruit of the Spirit
Gentleness

Gentleness: Softness of manners, mildness of temper; sweetness of disposition; meekness, tenderness, mild treatment.

"And the servant of the Lord must not strive; but be gentle unto all men, apt to teach, patient, In meekness instructing those that oppose themselves; if God peradventure will give them repentance to the acknowledging of the truth;" (2 Timothy 2:24-25)

"But the fruit of the Spirit is love, joy, peace, longsuffering, gentleness, goodness, faith, Meekness, temperance: against such there is no law." (Galatians 5:22-23)

"Put them in mind to be subject to principalities and powers, to obey magistrates, to be ready to every good work, To speak evil of no man, to be no brawlers, but gentle, shewing all meekness unto all men." (Titus 3:1-2)

When I was fearful, I believe the most effective way that I was treated was with gentleness. It was then that I had no fear. I don't speak of feigned gentleness, but gentleness with sincere concern for my welfare and my problems. When practical solutions to the problems were offered, this also helped. There have been many people I have met in my life who I considered to have a gentle spirit. I made sure to tell them. Some were offended, but I consider telling someone they have a gentle spirit to be a great compliment.

I met a clown once at a Creation Festival in 2004, and she had the gentlest spirit of anyone I have ever met. I told her she had a gentle spirit and we briefly discussed her spirit. She said her gentle spirit was especially effective when she visited children in hospitals. Her gentle spirit reached children where her partner's, which was much rougher, was not as effective with children. He reached other people with his spirit/personality, however.

Gentleness is a fruit of the spirit which we should all, as Christians, try to develop. Think of gentleness in your words and actions towards children and adults. I have been gentle at times, but also harsh in my speech at times, sometimes justified, and sometimes not. Both my wife and I need work on being less harsh and being gentler at times. With God's grace, we both will consistently achieve the gentleness God meant for us.

Other scriptures on gentleness:

"But the wisdom that is from above is first pure, then peaceable, gentle, and easy to be intreated, full of mercy and good fruits, without partiality, and without hypocrisy." (James 3:17)

"Now I Paul myself beseech you by the meekness and gentleness of Christ, who in presence am base among you, but being absent am bold toward you:" (2 Corinthians 10:1)

"Behold, the Lord God will come with strong hand, and his arm shall rule for him: behold, his reward is with him, and his work before him. He shall feed his flock like a shepherd: he shall gather the lambs with his arm, and carry them in his bosom, and shall gently lead those that are with young." (Isaiah 40:10-11)

Fruit of the Spirit
Faithfulness

Faithful: Firm in adherence to truth and the duties of religion; firmly adhering to duty; of true fidelity; loyal; true to allegiance; as a faithful subject.

Faithfulness: Fidelity; loyalty; firm adherence to allegiance and duty; truth, veracity; as the faithfulness of God.

"Know therefore that the Lord thy God, he is God, the faithful God, which keepeth covenant and mercy with them that love him and keep his commandments to a thousand generations;" (Deuteronomy 7:9)

"That I gave my brother Hanani, and Hananiah the ruler of the palace, charge over Jerusalem: for he was a faithful man, and feared God above many." (Nehemiah 7:2)

"He that is faithful in that which is least is faithful also in much: and he that is unjust in the least is unjust also in much." (Luke 16:10)

God's faithfulness is stronger than any man's, but some examples of men's faithfulness are as follows: Jonathan was a faithful friend to David. He risked his father, Saul's, wrath and warned David of Saul's intentions to slay him. I think of another faithful friend portrayed in the Lord of the Rings movies, Samwise Gamgee. Sam was a faithful friend of Frodo. Sam stood by, encouraged and comforted Frodo throughout their journey to destroy the evil ring. I have never seen such a strong depiction of a faithful, loyal friend. Sam stood by him through danger, evil and deceit, and at one point carried him on his back.

Other scriptures on faithfulness:

"And the heavens shall praise thy wonders, O Lord: thy faithfulness also in the congregation of the saints." (Psalm 89:5)

"Thy faithfulness is unto all generations: thou hast established the earth, and it abideth." (Psalm 119:90)

Fruit of the Spirit
Self-Control

Self-Control: Control of oneself or one's actions or feelings, etc.

Temperance: Moderation; particularly, habitual moderation in regard to the indulgence of the natural appetites and passions; restrained or moderate indulgence; as temperance in eating or drinking; temperate in pleasures; temperance in the indulgence of joy or mirth. Temperance in eating and drinking is opposed to gluttony and drunkenness, and in other indulgences, to excess. Patience, calmness, sedateness, moderation of passion. Temperate in speech.

"But Daniel purposed in his heart that he would not defile himself with the portion of the king's meat, nor with the wine which he drank: therefore he requested of the prince of the eunuchs that he might not defile himself." (Daniel 1:8)

"That the aged men be sober, grave, temperate, sound in faith, in charity, in patience." (Titus 2:2)

"He that loveth pleasure shall be a poor man: he that loveth wine and oil shall not be rich." (Proverbs 21:17)

A HIGHER STANDARD: ABSTAINING FROM DRINKING ALCOHOL

A general rule of thumb is to be moderate in the things we do, i.e. don't do things in excess. 1 Corinthians 9:25 says, "And every man that striveth for mastery (to win the race of life) be temperate in all things." However, there are indications that leaders should restrain from wine altogether as it defiles (pollutes or makes impure) the body. Wine, drunkenness, drinking: there are over 150 references to wine in the Bible.

Although God calls us to moderation or temperance, I believe the Bible calls leaders to a higher standard.

There are many examples within the Bible of this principle. In Leviticus 10:9 it called priests to abstain from wine or strong drink. It says, "Do not drink wine or strong drink, thou, nor thy sons with thee, when ye go into a tabernacle of the congregation, lest ye die: it shall be a statute forever throughout your generation."

The Nazarites were Israeli leaders. Sampson comes to mind. The Nazarites vowed to keep a number of laws to retain that leadership. One of the laws in Numbers 6:3 says, "He shall separate himself from wine and strong drink, and shall drink no vinegar or wine or vinegar or strong drink, neither shall he drink any liquor of grapes, nor moist grapes or dried. Proverbs 23:31-32 says, "Look not upon the wine when it is red, when it giveth his color in the cup, when it moveth itself aright. At the last it biteth like a serpent and stingeth like an adder."

Kings were called not to drink. Proverbs 31:4-7 says, "It is not for king, O Lemuel, it is not for kings to drink wine; nor princes strong drink. Lest they drink and forget the law and pervert the judgment of any of the afflicted. Give strong drink unto him that is ready to perish and wine unto them with heavy hearts. Let him drink and forget his poverty and remember his misery no more." Drinking will cause you to become insensible to the world around you. Not a good thing.

The Rechabites were of the Kenite family and were Israeli leaders. In Chapter 35 of Jeremiah the son of Jonadab followed their father's commandment not to drink wine. The sons said in Jeremiah 35:6 "We will drink no wine: for Jonadab the son of Rechab our father commanded us, saying, ye shall drink no wine, neither ye nor your sons forever." God honored the Rechabites, saying in Jeremiah 35:19, "Therefore thus saith the Lord of hosts, the God of Israel; Jonadab the son of Rechab shall not want a man to stand before me for ever.." God indicated all the descendants of Rechab would be in an honored position, i.e. serving God. They kept the commandment to honor their father and also lived up to a higher standard, i.e. not to drink wine.

John the Baptist also abstained from wine. Luke 1:15 says, "For he shall be great in the sight of the Lord, and shall drink neither wine nor strong drink; and he shall be filled with the Holy Ghost, even from his mother's womb."

TEMPERANCE: MODERATION IN DRINK: NOT TO EXCESS

There are many warnings against drunkenness.

"Wine is a mocker (someone who derides, ridicules, disappoints) strong drink is raging: and whosoever is deceived thereby is not wise." (Proverbs 20:1)

"Be not among winebibbers (one who drinks much wine), among riotous eaters of flesh." (Proverbs 23:20)

"Who hath woe? Who hath sorrow? Who hath contentions (arguments)? Who hath babbling? Who hath wounds without cause? Who hath redness of eyes? They that tarry long at the wine, they that go seek mixed wine." (Proverbs 23:29-30)

"Woe unto them that rise early in the morning, that they may follow strong drink; that continue until night, till wine inflame them!" (Isaiah 5:11)

"Woe unto him that giveth his neighbor drink, that puttest thy bottle to him, and makest him drunken also, that thou mayest look on their nakedness." (Habakkuk 2:15)

"Nor thieves, nor covetous, nor drunkards, nor revilers, nor extortioners, shall inherit the kingdom of God." (1 Corinthians 6:10)

"And be not drunk with wine, wherein is excess; but be filled with the spirit." (Ephesians 5:16)

"That the aged men be sober, grave, temperate, sound in faith, in charity in patience." (Titus 2:2)

"And every man that striveth for the mastery is temperate in all things..." (1 Corinthians 9:25)

BIBLICAL SIDE EFFECTS OF DRINKING OR DRINKING TO EXCESS

"Lest they drink, and forget the law, and pervert the judgment of any of the afflicted." (Proverbs 31:5)

"Give strong drink unto him that is ready to perish, and wine unto those that be of heavy hearts. Let him drink, and forget his poverty, and remember his misery no more." (Proverbs 31:6-7)

"But Daniel purposed in his heart that he would not defile himself with the portion of the king's meat, nor with the wine which he drank: therefore he requested of the prince of the eunuchs that he might not defile himself." (Daniel 1:8)

"Look not thou upon the wine when it is red, when it giveth his colour in the cup, when it moveth itself aright. At the last it biteth like a serpent, and stingeth like an adder." (Proverbs 23:31-32)

Other scriptures on temperance:

"Let your moderation be known unto all men. The Lord is at hand." (Philippians 4:5)

"And beside this, giving all diligence, add to your faith virtue; and to virtue knowledge;" (2 Peter 1:5)

Gifts of the Spirit
Motivational

Prophecy: Preaching; public interpretation of Scripture; exhortation or instruction.

Prophesy: In scripture, to preach; to instruct in religious doctrines; to interpret or explain Scripture or religious subjects: to exhort

Ministry: Agency; service; aid; interposition; instrumentality.

Teach: To instruct; to inform; to communicate to another the knowledge of that of which he was before ignorant.

Exhort: To give strength, spirit or courage; to encourage.

Rule: To govern; administer; lead; to control the will and actions of others, either by arbitrary power and authority or by established laws.

Mercy: Kindness in excess of what is fair.

Hospitality: The act or practice of receiving and entertaining strangers or guests without reward or with kind and generous liberality.

> "Having then gifts differing according to the grace that is given to us, whether prophecy, let us prophesy according to the proportion of faith; Or ministry, let us wait on our ministering: or he that teacheth, on teaching; Or he that exhorteth, on exhortation: he that giveth, let him do it with simplicity; he that ruleth, with diligence; he that sheweth mercy, with cheerfulness." (Romans 12:6-8)

> "Distributing to the necessity of saints; given to hospitality." (Romans 12:13)

The motivational gifts are those we are given at birth by the grace of God. Your gifts may increase by the grace of God. I believe I have two primary gifts, mercy and encouragement. My wife believes I have the gift of prophecy and I concur. To have the gift of mercy, one must be kind in excess of what is fair. Kindness has five elements to it: generosity, friendliness, sympathy, tender-heartedness and gentleness, all of these in excess of what is fair.

Encouragement is to come alongside and strengthen, to give courage to. There is nothing better than the word of God to strengthen people's spirits. The word of God is so full of knowledge and encouraging words. For instance, John 16:33 says, "in this world ye shall have tribulation, but be of good cheer; I have overcome the world."

In regard to prophecy, I love to preach to my children. I also like to preach publicly about scripture. I enjoy speaking about the word of God to the prison inmates. I love to instruct in the word. I believe this gift to be similar in some ways to teaching, but prophesying is instructing more on scriptural concepts.

Other scriptures on the gifts:

"And he gave some, apostles; and some, prophets; and some, evangelists; and some, pastors and teachers; For the perfecting of the saints, for the work of the ministry, for the edifying of the body of Christ:" (Ephesians 4:11-12)

"And he carried away all Jerusalem, and all the princes, and all the mighty men of valour, even ten thousand captives, and all the craftsmen and smiths: none remained, save the poorest sort of the people of the land." (2 Kings 24:14)

Gifts of the Spirit
Supernatural

Word of wisdom: The supernatural power to speak with divine insight, whether in solving difficult problems, defending the faith, resolving conflicts, giving practical advice or pleading one's case before hostile authorities.

Word of knowledge: The power to communicate information that is divinely revealed.

Faith: The supernatural ability to move mountains; to solve difficult problems by one's belief.

Heal: To cure of a disease or wound and restore to soundness, or to that state of body in which the natural functions are regularly performed; as to heal the sick.

Miracle: In theology, an event or effect contrary to the established constitution and course of things, or a deviation from the known laws of nature; a supernatural event. Miracles can be wrought only by Almighty power; as when Christ healed lepers saying "I will, be thou clean" and calmed the tempest "Peace, be still."

Prophecy: A person receives a direct revelation from God and transmits it to others; foretelling the future.

Discerning of spirits: The power to determine if a person is speaking by the Holy Spirit or by the devil.

Tongues: The ability to speak in a foreign language without having learned it.

Interpretation of tongues: The power to understand a language that the person has never known and convey it with local language.

"Now there are diversities of gifts, but the same Spirit." (1 Corinthians 12:4)

"For to one is given by the Spirit the word of wisdom; to another the word of knowledge by the same Spirit; To another faith by the same Spirit; to another the gifts of healing by the same Spirit; To another the working of miracles; to another prophecy; to another discerning of spirits; to another divers kinds of tongues; to another the interpretation of tongues." (1 Corinthians 12:8-10)

The supernatural gifts come from the Holy Spirit. They are here today as they were in Christ's time, and before. The Holy Spirit endows people with these gifts as He chooses to edify others. In our church, we often hear the gift of tongues and interpretation of tongues. We, being many, are one body in Christ; every single one, members of one another, and loving each other. We are to covet earnestly the best gifts, but a more excellent way is to have or show love.

Instructive Spirit

Instruct: To teach; to inform the mind.

Reproof: Blame expressed to the face; censure for a fault

Rebuke: To chide; to reprove; to reprehend (blame) for a fault; to chasten.

Chasten: To purify from errors or faults.

> "Whoso loveth instruction loveth knowledge: but he that hateth reproof is brutish." (Proverbs 12:1)

> "He is in the way of life that keepeth instruction: but he that refuseth reproof erreth." (Proverbs 10:17)

> "Open rebuke is better than secret love. Faithful are the wounds of a friend; but the kisses of an enemy are deceitful." (Proverbs 27:5-6)

There is a place for constructive criticism/rebuke/reproof/ chastening in the Christian way of life. We as Christians are to receive these rebukes and learn from them. In my life, I have accepted some rebukes well and some not so well – due to their frequency (what I call harping). Rebukes may hurt but a Christian counselor once told me nobody said the truth wouldn't hurt. It's true that rebukes and reproofs do hurt, but if we learn from them, God is pleased.

However, when someone is overly critical, the constructive criticism begins to fall on deaf ears, and can also harm a relationship. How much is too much rebuke? I asked this of the Christian counselor and he said 90% of the time the Bible talks of loving others, being kind, merciful, forgiving, encouraging, and edifying others. Only 10% of the time does it talk about rebuke, reproof, or chastening of others. This mathematical formula is a good guideline but not foolproof on a case-by-case basis.

I believe our attitude, in general, should be one of love, kindness, and encouragement. Though if the words or action of someone bothers us so much, we should speak to the person as it says in Matthew 18:15, "Moreover if thy brother shall trespass against thee, go and tell him his fault between thee and him alone: if he shall hear thee, thou hast gained thy brother." Another important concept this counselor passed on to me was that if you constructively criticize someone, you must be willing to come alongside that person and help them with their fault.

More scripture on instruction via rebuke/reproof:

"This witness is true. Wherefore rebuke them sharply, that they may be sound in the faith;" (Titus 1:13)

Strength of Spirit

Strength: Power or vigor of any kind. Strength there must be to either love or war. Power of mind, intellectual force; the power of any faculty; as strength of memory, strength of reason; strength of judgment. Spirit, animation. Me thinks I feel new strength arise within me.

Spirit: The soul of man; the intelligent immaterial and immortal part of human beings. Ecclesiastes 12:7 says, "The spirit of man shall return to God that gave it."

Soul: The spiritual, rational and immortal substance in man, which distinguishes him from brutes; that part of man which enables him to think and reason, and renders him a subject of moral government. The immortality of the soul is a fundamental article of the Christian system. Such is the nature of the human soul, that it must have a God, an object of supreme affection.

> "The Lord is my strength and song, and he is become my salvation: he is my God, and I will prepare him a habitation; my father's God, and I will exalt him." (Exodus 15:2)

> " Be of good courage, and he shall strengthen your heart, all ye that hope in the Lord." (Psalm 31:24)

> "Nevertheless I am continually with thee: thou hast holden me by my right hand." (Psalm 73:23)

> "My flesh and my heart faileth: but God is the strength of my heart, and my portion for ever." (Psalm 73:26)

The Lord is my strength and salvation. There are times when I feel my spiritual strength has ebbed and I go to the Lord's word and I am renewed. His word, writing about His word, and His truths give me purpose. As I write this, I have had another problem with medication. It is very discouraging that medication that is meant to help the body has such harmful effects. As I deal with these problems, my spiritual strength has been low and I've needed renewal from my Lord.

For whatever reason, God allowed me to experience these detrimental effects. A song I've come to love, to identify with, and which encouraged me is, "God is the Strength of My Heart." It goes like this: "Whom have I in heaven but you. There is nothing on earth I desire beside you. My heart and my strength many times they fail but there is one truth that always will prevail. God is the strength of my heart. God is the strength of my heart. God is the strength of my heart and my portion forever. God is the strength of my heart. God is the strength of my heart and my portion forever. My peace, my joy forever." The truth of this song is so strong in my heart that it permeates my soul. My heart and my strength do often fail. God is always there watching over me, loving me, causing me to grow. He is my strength and my portion (a part of me) forever. I see God holding my hand as a friend, and comforting me during difficult times.

Other scriptures on spiritual strength:

"In the day when I cried thou answeredst me, and strengthenedst me with strength in my soul." (Psalm 138:3)

"Then he said unto them, Go your way, eat the fat, and drink the sweet, and send portions unto them for whom nothing is prepared: for this day is holy unto our Lord: neither be ye sorry; for the joy of the Lord is your strength." (Nehemiah 8:10)

"The way of the Lord is strength to the upright: but destruction shall be to the workers of iniquity." (Proverbs 10:29)

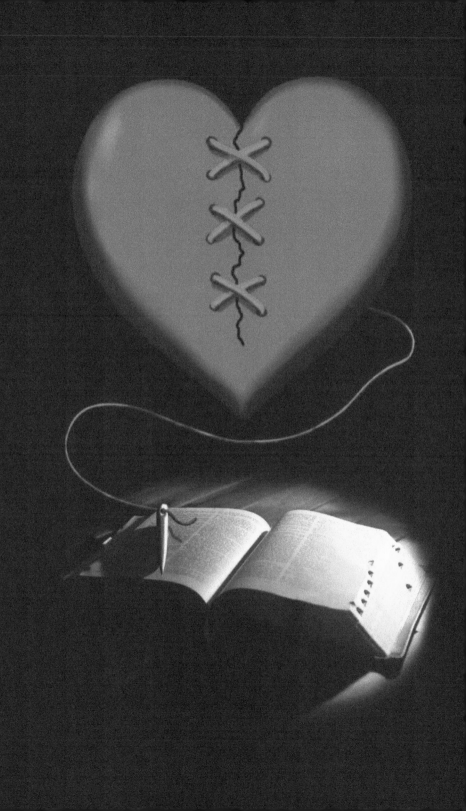

HEALING

ᘓᘐ

Heal: To cure of a disease or wound and restore to sound-ness, or to that state of body (mind and emotions) in which the natural functions are regularly performed; as to heal the sick. To cure; to make whole or healthy.

Cure: To restoration to health.

Health: A condition in which all functions of body and mind are normally active.

> "And it came to pass, that after three days they found him in the temple, sitting in the midst of the doctors, both hear-ing them, and asking them questions." (Luke 2:46)

> "The centurion answered and said, Lord, I am not wor-thy that thou shouldest come under my roof: but speak the word only, and my servant shall be healed." (Matthew 8:8)

> "And said, If thou wilt diligently hearken to the voice of the Lord thy God, and wilt do that which is right in his sight, and wilt give ear to his commandments, and keep all his statutes, I will put none of these diseases upon thee, which I have brought upon the Egyptians: for I am the Lord that healeth thee." (Exodus 15:26)

My mother-in-law has had great interest in healing. I have too –
in regards to healing of the emotions, mind, and spirit. I write
this section in honor of her. Over the years Marge has shared
with me a number of scriptures which I believe, if claimed in
faith, can bring healing to the body, mind, and soul. If we have
faith and don't doubt, God can do miraculous healings. As I
write this, our pastor's daughter gave testimony that she has
been healed from a suffering she has been experiencing for
many years. Our church has been praying for her diligently
for healing. Her healing took place after visiting the Brooklyn
Tabernacle where they also prayed for her. Prior to the healing,
the pastor had testified that she had been to 21 doctors.

It is my belief that God placed doctors on the earth to
help heal people. Because man is made in God's image, he is
extremely creative and has made wonderful inroads into medicine and healing the sick. I believe some in the profession are
specifically called of God, into the healing profession. Yet there
are some illnesses/wounds beyond that of human doctors, which
God miraculously heals. God is a good God, a healing God.

Some of the scriptures my mother-in-law gave me on healing are as follows:

> "For mine Angel shall go before thee, and bring thee in
> unto the Amorites, and the Hittites, and the Perizzites, and
> the Canaanites, the Hivites, and the Jebusites: and I will
> cut them off. Thou shalt not bow down to their gods, nor
> serve them, nor do after their works: but thou shalt utterly
> overthrow them, and quite break down their images. And
> ye shall serve the Lord your God, and he shall bless thy
> bread, and thy water; and I will take sickness away from
> the midst of thee." (Exodus 23:23-25)

> "He sent his word, and healed them, and delivered them
> from their destructions." (Psalm 107:20)

> "Bless the Lord, O my soul, and forget not all his benefits:
> Who forgiveth all thine iniquities; who healeth all thy dis-
> eases;" (Psalms 103:2-3)

"Christ hath redeemed us from the curse of the law, being made a curse for us: for it is written, Cursed is every one that hangeth on a tree:" (Galatians 3:13)

"Surely he hath borne our griefs, and carried our sorrows: yet we did esteem him stricken, smitten of God, and afflicted. But he was wounded for our transgressions, he was bruised for our iniquities: the chastisement of our peace was upon him; and with his stripes we are healed. All we like sheep have gone astray; we have turned every one to his own way; and the Lord hath laid on him the iniquity of us all." (Isaiah 53:4-6)

"That it might be fulfilled which was spoken by Esaias the prophet, saying, Himself took our infirmities, and bare our sicknesses." (Matthew 8:17)

"Is any sick among you? let him call for the elders of the church; and let them pray over him, anointing him with oil in the name of the Lord:" (James 5:14)

"And he came down with them, and stood in the plain, and the company of his disciples, and a great multitude of people out of all Judaea and Jerusalem, and from the sea coast of Tyre and Sidon, which came to hear him, and to be healed of their diseases; And they that were vexed with unclean spirits: and they were healed. And the whole multitude sought to touch him: for there went virtue out of him, and healed them all." (Luke 6:17-19)

"They shall take up serpents; and if they drink any deadly thing, it shall not hurt them; they shall lay hands on the sick, and they shall recover." (Mark 16:18)

"And the eyes of them that see shall not be dim, and the ears of them that hear shall hearken." (Isaiah 32:3)

Church

In the Bible, the church is the people, not just a building. My pastor calls the church a hospital for the soul. Scripture professed in church is healing. Godly music is healing and worship is healing. By recognizing the greatness of God, exalting Him and showing our gratitude to Him for a good and abundant life, we are healed. We can cast our cares on Him.

> "And I say also unto thee, That thou art Peter, and upon this rock I will build my church; and the gates of hell shall not prevail against it." (Matthew 16:18)

> "And when the day of Pentecost was fully come, they were all with one accord in one place. And suddenly there came a sound from heaven as of a rushing mighty wind, and it filled all the house where they were sitting. And there appeared unto them cloven tongues like as of fire, and it sat upon each of them." (Acts 2:1-3)

> "Is any sick among you? let him call for the elders of the church; and let them pray over him, anointing him with oil in the name of the Lord:" (James 5:14)

There is no perfect church. The church is made up of imperfect people. Jesus said you would know them by their love. A loving church is a good church, one that lifts the word of God, and Jesus is a good church. One in which there is no backbiting is a good church. My church is my second family. In my recent significant problems, I lost my toe and could not drive, my mother died, and I had family problems – 21 people either offered to help me, visited me in the hospital and rehab facility, or did help me by driving me to doctor's appointments. This love and support got me through a difficult time. Praise God for church friends in times of need!

Other scriptures regarding the church:

"Not forsaking the assembling of ourselves together, as the manner of some is; but exhorting one another: and so much the more, as ye see the day approaching." (Hebrews 10:25)

"And thus are the secrets of his heart made manifest; and so falling down on his face he will worship God, and report that God is in you of a truth." (1 Corinthians 14:25)

"And Saul was consenting unto his death. And at that time there was a great persecution against the church which was at Jerusalem; and they were all scattered abroad throughout the regions of Judaea and Samaria, except the apostles." (Acts 8:1)

Healing Through Death

Death: The state of being, animal or vegetable, in which there is a total and permanent cessation of all vital functions.

Comment: People are meant to live a full and abundant life. Any philosophy or theology that suggests taking a life before God calls them to heaven, such as abortion, assisted suicide, suicide, murder, etc. is wrong. God hates the shedding of innocent blood.

Heaven: Among Christians, the part in space in which the omnipresent Jehovah is supposed to afford more sensible manifestations of his glory. Hence this is called the habitation of God; and is represented as the residence of angels and blessed spirits.

Eulogy: Praise; a speech or writing in commendation of a person on account of his/her valuable qualities or services.

> "So when this corruptible shall have put on incorruption, and this mortal shall have put on immortality, then shall be brought to pass the saying that is written, Death is swallowed up in victory. O death, where is thy sting? O grave, where is thy victory?" (1 Corinthians 15:54-55)

> "But as touching the resurrection of the dead, have ye not read that which was spoken unto you by God, saying, I am the God of Abraham, and the God of Isaac, and the God of Jacob? God is not the God of the dead, but of the living." (Matthew 22:31-32)

> "That as sin hath reigned unto death, even so might grace reign through righteousness unto eternal life by Jesus Christ our Lord." (Romans 5:21)

When a Christian goes to heaven, death is the ultimate healing. While in heaven for eternity, there will be no tears,

pain, or suffering; it will be life in paradise. Jesus has prepared for us a mansion in heaven. Part of dying, the burial
and the grave, is also the eulogies expressed for the dead.
These eulogies are also healing for those who remain on
earth. I would like to share the eulogies of my mother and
father.

My mother was loving, kind, and my friend. I've said
often that my parents were one of God's greatest blessings
to me. I once questioned my mother's faith, and my dad said
to me you are underestimating your mother. He was right,
her faith was strong. My mom used to kid my dad when he
nervously clicked his fingers on the table. She said he was
the fiddler on the roof. I have fond memories of my mother's
servant attitude, like serving me cocoa and toast for breakfast. My mom didn't like to go to Canada with my dad, my
brother, sister and me, but she never prevented or discouraged us from going. She gave us the freedom to enjoy our
vacation in Canada. She was a strong woman who loved her
family.

I feel I must preface what I'm about to say about my dad
that no man is without faults. But I would like to say a few
things about my dad. He was generous, and the friendliest
man I knew. He was kind and loved his children and people
greatly. He was bold and courageous. He was an intelligent
man. He was a good man to seek counsel from. His character
was an example to be followed. He, as a godly man, was a
man to be respected. I have said to others that I believe my
parents to be one of God's greatest blessings to me. He showed
me a great example to follow in life, especially with his generosity and love. We experienced many adventures together;
Canada, canoeing on the Susquehanna River, our woodland;
memories I will never forget. A friend of ours said to me more
than once, you don't know how fortunate you are to have
the parents you do. It's true. I haven't seen the darker side
of parental life, but I think I know how good of a father and
mother I have had.

Other scriptures on death, eternal life in heaven:

"For God so loved the world, that he gave his only begotten Son, that whosoever believeth in him should not perish, but have everlasting life." (John 3:16)

"In my Father's house are many mansions: if it were not so, I would have told you. I go to prepare a place for you." (John 14:2)

"And these shall go away into everlasting punishment: but the righteous into life eternal." (Matthew 25:46)

Healing Through Doctors

Doctor: A physician; one whose occupation is to cure diseases.

Physician: A person skilled in the art of healing; one whose profession is to prescribe remedies for diseases. In a spiritual sense, one that heals moral diseases; as a person that heals the human soul.

Psychologist: A person that heals the human soul through counseling.

Psychiatrist: One who dispenses medicine for psychological disorders.

> "But when Jesus heard that, he said unto them, They that be whole need not a physician, but they that are sick." (Matthew 9:12)

> "Luke, the beloved physician, and Demas, greet you." (Colossians 4:14)

> "And a woman having an issue of blood twelve years, which had spent all her living upon physicians, neither could be healed of any," (Luke 8:43)

I have had good and bad experiences with doctors, but mostly good. I believe many doctors called to the position have the gift of healing. I am grateful to a number of godly doctors, my podiatrist (foot doctor), my psychologist, my psychiatrist, and my family physician. They have had a positive impact on my life. My podiatrist saved my life from gangrene of the toe. My psychologist led me to salvation and provided practical solutions to my problems. My psychiatrist led me to a medication that stabilized my emotions. My family physician watches over my health regularly. I am grateful to them and my Lord for leading me to them. God is the great physician and can heal us miraculously.

Other Scriptures on doctors, physicians, healers:

"Heal me, O Lord, and I shall be healed; save me, and I shall be saved: for thou art my praise." (Jeremiah 17:14)

"I said, Lord, be merciful unto me: heal my soul; for I have sinned against thee." (Psalm 41:4)

"And said, If thou wilt diligently hearken to the voice of the Lord thy God, and wilt do that which is right in his sight, and wilt give ear to his commandments, and keep all his statutes, I will put none of these diseases upon thee, which I have brought upon the Egyptians: for I am the Lord that healeth thee." (Exodus 15:26)

Luke 15:11-32 - "...for this your brother was dead, and is alive; he was lost, and is found."

Healing Through Forgiveness

Forgiveness: The act of forgiving; the pardon of an offender, by which he is treated as not guilty.

Forgive: To pardon; to remit, as an offense, to overlook an offense, and treat the offender as not guilty; To forgive the offense; send it away; to reject it, that is, not to impute it to the offender. To overlook a transgression; to let go of.

> "And the son said unto him, Father, I have sinned against heaven, and in thy sight, and am no more worthy to be called thy son. But the father said to his servants, Bring forth the best robe, and put it on him; and put a ring on his hand, and shoes on his feet: And bring hither the fatted calf, and kill it; and let us eat, and be merry: For this my son was dead, and is alive again; he was lost, and is found. And they began to be merry." (Luke 15:21-24)

> "As far as the east is from the west, so far hath he removed our transgressions from us." (Psalm 103:12)

> "And they shall teach no more every man his neighbour, and every man his brother, saying, Know the Lord: for they shall all know me, from the least of them unto the greatest of them, saith the Lord: for I will forgive their iniquity, and I will remember their sin no more." (Jeremiah 31:34)

The story of the prodigal son is one of the best stories of forgiveness and love. The father's forgiveness healed their relationship. God, in the wisdom of His word, shows that we should forgive the hurt and sins of others against us and remember them no more.

The hurts, the pain of cruel words, experiences, and sins against us, often repeat themselves in our minds. If we let them continue in our minds and hearts, they can have a devastating effect on our mind and emotions. I've heard people say, it is possible to forgive or pardon a person, but not forget the hurt or the sin. I contend, however, that with God all things are possible. I've found that if you make a decision to forgive, and claim Psalm 103:12 and Jeremiah 31:34, the pain of those hurts and the repetition of those sins against us are erased from our memory/mind, therefore, healing our minds and emotions. Forgiveness is not always easy, especially when one of the Ten Commandments is committed against us. I often need God's help to forgive.

Other scriptures on forgiveness:

"For a multitude of the people, even many of Ephraim, and Manasseh, Issachar, and Zebulun, had not cleansed themselves, yet did they eat the passover otherwise than it was written. But Hezekiah prayed for them, saying, The good Lord pardon every one That prepareth his heart to seek God, the Lord God of his fathers, though he be not cleansed according to the purification of the sanctuary. And the Lord hearkened to Hezekiah, and healed the people." (2 Chronicles 30:18-20)

" I, even I, am he that blotteth out thy transgressions for mine own sake, and will not remember thy sins." (Isaiah 43:25)

Comment: When we forgive, it is not only for the sake of the person who sinned against us but more for our own sake; for our own healing, and so that our Father in heaven will also forgive our sins.

Healing Power of a Hug

Hug: To press close in an embrace. To embrace closely. To hold fast; to treat with fondness.

Embrace: To take, clasp or enclose in the arms; to press to the bosom, in token of affection.

> "And when he came to himself, he said, How many hired servants of my father's have bread enough and to spare, and I perish with hunger! I will arise and go to my father, and will say unto him, Father, I have sinned against heaven, and before thee, And am no more worthy to be called thy son: make me as one of thy hired servants. And he arose, and came to his father. But when he was yet a great way off, his father saw him, and had compassion, and ran, and fell on his neck, and kissed him." (Luke 15:17-20)

My wife has said a hug is worth a thousand words. My daughter delights in group hugs. Our parents give us hugs freely. As seen in the story of the prodigal son, the embracing of his father showed his son his love, forgiveness, and acceptance of him back into the family and home. God, in the wisdom of His word, gave us an example of how to heal/reconcile broken relationships, hurt feelings, and how to show our sons and daughters that we love them, and accept them even with their faults and mistakes. That's a great example of how our Father in heaven is, eagerly waiting with open arms to accept us into His kingdom. God is not willing that any should perish, but that all would have eternal joy in heaven through the acceptance and belief in Christ, who showed us the depth of His love by His sacrificial death on the cross.

Other scriptures on hugs/embraces:

> "To every thing there is a season, and a time to every purpose under the heaven:" (Ecclesiastes 3:1)

"A time to cast away stones, and a time to gather stones together; a time to embrace, and a time to refrain from embracing;" (Ecclesiastes 3:5)

"And he said, Is not he rightly named Jacob? for he hath supplanted me these two times: he took away my birthright; and, behold, now he hath taken away my blessing. And he said, Hast thou not reserved a blessing for me?" (Genesis 27:36)

"And Esau hated Jacob because of the blessing wherewith his father blessed him: and Esau said in his heart, The days of mourning for my father are at hand; then will I slay my brother Jacob." (Genesis 27:41)

"And Esau ran to meet him, and embraced him, and fell on his neck, and kissed him: and they wept." (Genesis 33:4)

Comment: This is the condensed version of the story of Jacob and Esau. I recommend you go to Genesis for the whole story.

Healing Through Humor

Humorous: Containing humor; full of wild or fanciful images; adapted to excite laughter; jocular; playful.

Merriment: Mirth, gayety with laughter..

Merry: Causing laughter or mirth, delightful; jovial; pleasant; agreeable.

Laughter: Convulsive merriment, an expression of mirth peculiar to man.

Mirth: Social merriment, hilarity, high excitement of pleasurable feelings in company.

> "A merry heart doeth good like a medicine: but a broken spirit drieth the bones." (Proverbs 17:22)

Merriment, humor, and laughter are very healing to the mind and emotions. My dad recently went through an operation where they removed most of his nose because of skin cancer. But my dad is amazing. Through the pain and adversity of the operation, he was still joking. He was exhausted from the surgery, so my wife suggested he have a wheelchair. While in the wheelchair, his way was blocked by another wheelchair. Dad said "woo woo," like a train to get them to move. My Dad's humor comes naturally to him, and I believe it's because he loves people so much.

While walking Pumpkin, my dog, one day, we came across another dog, and his first instinct was one of conflict. I spoke to Pumpkin to try to teach him some rules on conflict resolution. I said to him, "If it be possible, as much as lieth in – be at peace with all" (Romans 12:18) dogs . He calmed down almost immediately.

Other scriptures on mirth/merry/laughter:

> "A merry heart maketh a cheerful countenance: but by sorrow of the heart the spirit is broken." (Proverbs 15:13)

"For there they that carried us away captive required of us a song; and they that wasted us required of us mirth, saying, Sing us one of the songs of Zion." (Psalm 137:3)

"To every thing there is a season, and a time to every purpose under the heaven:" (Ecclesiastes 3:1)

"A time to weep, and a time to laugh; a time to mourn, and a time to dance;" (Ecclesiastes 3:4)

Healing Through the Love of a Pet

Pet: A fondling; any little animal fondled and indulged.

Dog: A species of quadrupeds, belonging to the genus Canis, of many varieties, as the mastiff, the hound, the spaniel, the shepherd's dog, the terrier, the harrier, the bloodhound, etc.

> "And there was a certain beggar named Lazarus, which was laid at his gate, full of sores, And desiring to be fed with the crumbs which fell from the rich man's table: moreover the dogs came and licked his sores." (Luke 16:20-21)

When I was going through my divorce I was very alone. During this time, I felt so very close to my dog, a sheltie named Rusty. The love and loyalty of my dog helped me through a very difficult time. Rusty lived to be seventeen and when he had to be put to sleep it was a sad time for me. Next, I got a terrier named Pumpkin. He weighed about eight pounds and we walked every morning. At night, he sat on my lap as I watch TV and he slept with us in bed. The wonderful gift God had given me in Pumpkin is that I have Diabetes and have numbness in my feet. Pumpkin licked my feet and gave me comfort. My wife was very good with him and took care of most of his needs. She fed him, gave him water, brushed his teeth, gave him play/cuddle time, and had found the best kennel ever – which was even air-conditioned.. Sounds a little extravagant, but the cost is also reasonable. My wife even communicated with him. She would say to him "did you like that piece of meat" and he would lick his chops.

I believe it is known that the elderly and those very sick are lifted up and healed emotionally, and their loneliness is healed from the love and loyalty of a dog or cat. God has provided us a wonderful gift in our pets.

In the story "Old Yeller," a boy came to love Old Yeller very much for his loyalty, love, and bravery when he protected his family from a bear, wolves, and raccoons. When Old Yeller contracted rabies, the boy courageously shot the dog. It was the hardest thing he had ever done. His dad wisely spoke to him, saying that he was proud of how he handled it. Then he said bad things happen in life but there are also a lot of good times and if we worry too long about the bad things, we'll never enjoy life. Then he told him a little secret. When you lose something very dear to you, replace it with something else that is good and loveable. The story ended with the boy accepting one of Old Yeller's puppies.

A week after I wrote this, I found out that Pumpkin had slipped out the door and run away. My daughter, who is six years old, had taken off his collar that had his license on. Many prayers had gone up to heaven. The next day I decided to go to the Humane Society and give them a picture of Pumpkin so they would recognize him if he came in. As I was driving into the Humane Society driveway, there was Pumpkin, on a leash, being walked by a woman. A man had taken him there only an hour or two after he had run away. They had wormed him, given him shots, and a flea treatment. This also was a blessing in disguise, in that he was soon due all of those things and their cost was significantly less than the vets. Our prayers were answered, Praise be the name of the Lord.

Other scriptures on pets, dogs, animals:

"A greyhound; and he goat also; and a king, against whom there is no rising up." (Proverbs 30:31)

"A righteous man regardeth the life of his beast: but the tender mercies of the wicked are cruel." (Proverbs 12:10)

"I have made the earth, the man and the beast that are upon the ground, by my great power and by my outstretched arm, and have given it unto whom it seemed meet unto me." (Jeremiah 27:5)

Healing Through Medicine

Medicine: Any substance; liquid or solid that has the property of curing or mitigating disease in animals. Simple plants and minerals furnish most of our medicine. Even poisons used with judgment and in moderation are safe and efficacious medicines.

Balm: Anything which heals, or which soothes or mitigates pain.

> "And by the river upon the bank thereof, on this side and on that side, shall grow all trees for meat, whose leaf shall not fade, neither shall the fruit thereof be consumed: it shall bring forth new fruit according to his months, because their waters they issued out of the sanctuary: and the fruit thereof shall be for meat, and the leaf thereof for medicine." (Ezekiel 47:12)

> "Is there no balm in Gilead; is there no physician there? why then is not the health of the daughter of my people recovered?" (Jeremiah 8:22)

> "Babylon is suddenly fallen and destroyed: howl for her; take balm for her pain, if so be she may be healed." (Jeremiah 51:8)

By God's grace, my bipolar disorder has been healed by medicine, specifically Abilify. I also attribute my healing to prayer and the word of God. My emotions were up and down but God healed me through this medicine. I am also healed of my diabetes through medicine, specifically insulin. I must remain vigilant in taking the medicine. I believe it is God's will that we live a whole, abundant life. My gratitude is to God first and then to my doctor's prescription and pharmaceutical companies that produced these medicines. Medication often has side effects. I prayed often that the medication would only do what it was supposed to do. With God, all things are possible. There is hope for people with bipolar disorder and diabetes. Thanks be to God.

Other scriptures on medicines/balm:

"Judah, and the land of Israel, they were thy merchants: they traded in thy market wheat of Minnith, and Pannag, and honey, and oil, and balm." (Ezekiel 27:17)

"And their father Israel said unto them, If it must be so now, do this; take of the best fruits in the land in your vessels, and carry down the man a present, a little balm, and a little honey, spices, and myrrh, nuts, and almonds:" (Genesis 43:11)

Healing Through Music

Music: Melody or harmony; any succession of sounds so modulated as to please the ear, or any combination of simultaneous sounds in accordance or harmony. Music is vocal or instrumental. Vocal music is the melody of a single voice, or the harmony of two or more voices in concert. Instrumental music is that produced by one or more instruments.

Song: In general, that which is sung or uttered with musical modulations of the voice, whether of the human voice or that of a bird.

Psalm: A sacred song or hymn; a song composed on a divine subject and in praise of God.

> "And it came to pass as they came, when David was returned from the slaughter of the Philistine, that the women came out of all cities of Israel, singing and dancing, to meet king Saul, with tabrets, with joy, and with instruments of musick." (1 Samuel 18:6)

> "Let our lord now command thy servants, which are before thee, to seek out a man, who is a cunning player on an harp: and it shall come to pass, when the evil spirit from God is upon thee, that he shall play with his hand, and thou shalt be well." (1 Samuel 16:16)

My personal experience with godly music is that it soothes the soul and heals the broken-hearted. Christian song lyrics like "I am the God that Healeth thee, I am the Lord Your healer" come to mind. Music can heal by lifting one's spirit. It can soften the heart. Some of my favorites are: "God Can Make a Way"; "Unto Us a Child is Born"; and "It's a Wonderful World." They all have a healing aspect to them through their music and the word of truth they portray.

Other scriptures on music:

"Praise him with the sound of the trumpet: praise him with the psaltery and harp. Praise him with the timbrel and dance: praise him with stringed instruments and organs. Praise him upon the loud cymbals: praise him upon the high sounding cymbals." (Psalm 150:3-5)

"The Lord is my strength and song, and is become my salvation." (Psalm 118:14)

Healing Through Prayer

Pray: In worship, to address the Supreme Being (God) with solemnity and reverence, with adoration, confession of sins, supplication for mercy, and thanksgiving for blessings received.

> "Is any sick among you? let him call for the elders of the church; and let them pray over him, anointing him with oil in the name of the Lord: And the prayer of faith shall save the sick, and the Lord shall raise him up; and if he have committed sins, they shall be forgiven him. Confess your faults one to another, and pray one for another, that ye may be healed. The effectual fervent prayer of a righteous man availeth much." (James 5:14-16)

Prayer in the name of the Lord Jesus Christ is powerful. An easy way to remember the definition of pray is the acronym ACTS: Adoration, Confession, Thanksgiving and Supplication. We should often tell the Lord how much we adore him. If we confess our sins, He is faithful and just to forgive us our sins. We should always be thankful for who God is and what He has done for us, and finally we request our needs through supplication. If we don't know how to pray we can just say "Jesus, Jesus." We can also request the Holy Spirit to pray for us. Jesus is on the throne intervening on our behalf.

Other scriptures on prayer:

> "Ye ask, and receive not, because ye ask amiss, that ye may consume it upon your lusts." (James 4:3)

> "And he spake a parable unto them to this end, that men ought always to pray, and not to faint; Saying, There was in a city a judge, which feared not God, neither regarded man: And there was a widow in that city; and she came unto him, saying, Avenge me of mine adversary." (Luke 18:1-3)

"Yet because this widow troubleth me, I will avenge her, lest by her continual coming she weary me." (Luke 18:5)

"And shall not God avenge his own elect, which cry day and night unto him, though he bear long with them?" (Luke 18:7)

Comment: Please read the parable of the persistent widow in Luke 18.

Healing Through the Word of God

Word: The scripture; divine revelation or any part of it.

Broken-hearted: Having the spirits depressed or crushed by grief or despair.

> "The Spirit of the Lord is upon me, because he hath anointed me to preach the gospel to the poor; he hath sent me to heal the brokenhearted, to preach deliverance to the captives, and recovering of sight to the blind, to set at liberty them that are bruised," (Luke 4:18)

> "For the word of God is quick, and powerful, and sharper than any twoedged sword, piercing even to the dividing asunder of soul and spirit, and of the joints and marrow, and is a discerner of the thoughts and intents of the heart." (Hebrews 4:12)

Who are the broken-hearted? Those whose emotions have been shattered, their minds confused and their spirits crushed. God and Jesus had a heart for those who were broken. It is through our brokenness that we are humbled enough to see the Glory of God; to praise Him; worship Him with all our heart, mind, soul, and strength. God is a healing God. By His stripes we are healed. By His death on the cross, He took all of our sins and shame upon Himself so that we are white as snow. He imputed (transferred) His righteousness to us. Although, the word of God did not heal me by itself, it was a step in the right direction. I believe His word, prayer, medicine, and doctors brought about the healing of my broken heart.

Other scriptures on the word of God and healing:

> "So shall my word be that goeth forth out of my mouth: it shall not return unto me void, but it shall accomplish that which I please, and it shall prosper in the thing whereto I sent it." (Isaiah 55:11)

"If my people, which are called by my name, shall humble themselves, and pray, and seek my face, and turn from their wicked ways; then will I hear from heaven, and will forgive their sin, and will heal their land." (2 Chronicles 7:14)

EPILOGUE

CR

As I wrote this book, I sought the counsel of my wife, my father-in-law and mother-in-law, and my brother; all who I count as wiser than myself. One of my father-in-law's comments was "It's fine to write about these things, but you must live them." That's exactly what the definition of wisdom is— the right exercise or use of knowledge. I have a long way to go, but with God all things are possible.

My bipolar illness lasted over 20 years and my diabetes over 15 years. I guess you could say it was my time in the desert. Many times, I've said to myself, things can't be as bad as I feel, as I tried to get a grip on reality, and they weren't. They weren't because we have a God in heaven who loves us, cares about us, and wants the best for us. Also, there are many people who love and care about us enough to help us through our trouble. My healing has occurred over 30 or more years of my life. James 4:2-3 says, "...yet ye have not because ye ask not. Ye ask not and receive not because ye ask amiss," For those who may have similar struggles, our God is a loving God who wants to fill our heart's desires. Ask Him for healing, but wait patiently for His timing. God wants to complete a work in you so that His glory may be manifested. Jeremiah 29:11-13 says, "For I know the thoughts that I think toward you, saith the Lord, thoughts of peace, and not of evil, to give you an expected end. Then shall ye call upon me, and ye shall go and pray unto me, and I will hearken unto you. And ye shall seek me, and find me, when ye shall search for me with all your heart."

One of my favorite songs is "Glory to You" by Steve Green. This song not only applies to the knowledge presented in this book, but to my life. Some of the words are as follows: "What do I possess that You did not give to me? What mysteries are clear to me that You did not explain? When did I share truth that I did not receive from You? What good works did I perform that You did not ordain? Any strength I have, any good I do, comes from the life I've found in You…"

My last words are for those who love the Lord with all their heart, mind, soul and strength. There is hope for healing, no matter how grave things may seem. Nothing is impossible for God.

INDEX

ABOUT THE AUTHOR

Terry Busler was born in York, PA, and lived most of his life in Central Pennsylvania. He graduated from Penn State with a BA in the Russian language, worked as a civilian for the Navy for 35 years, and is now retired. In 1978, he had a breakdown due to the pressures of a bad marriage, being flooded out by Hurricane Eloise, and the Three Mile Island disaster. Due to the breakdown, he was diagnosed as bipolar and experienced most of the 24 emotions identified in his book and in the Bible. With the help of a godly psychologist he was saved. By studying the Bible, prayer, godly doctors, and diligently taking his medicine, he was/is healed of his bipolar disorder.